GENDER DISCRIMINATION IN THE KASHMIR VALLEY
(A Survey of Budgam and Baramulla Districts)

GENDER DISCRIMINATION IN THE KASHMIR VALLEY

(A Survey of Budgam and Baramulla Districts)

Bashir Ahmad Dabla
Sandeep K. Nayak
Khurshid-Ul-Islam

GYAN PUBLISHING HOUSE
NEW DELHI - 110002

GENDER DISCRIMINATION IN THE KASHMIR VALLEY

(A Survey of Budgam and Baramulla Districts)

ISBN : 81-212-0750-9

Published in 2000 in India by
Gyan Publishing House
5, Ansari Road
New Delhi 110 002
Phone : 3282060, 3261060 Fax : 3285914
E-mail : gyanbook@del2.vsnl.net.in
Visit Our Website At http:\\www.gyanbooks.com

Laser Typesetting: Grow Computers, Delhi
Printed at: Mehra Offset Press, New Delhi

CONTENTS

List of Tables 7

Foreward 13

Preface 23

1. Introduction 27
2. Women and Society: Views about Gender Discrimination 39
3. Methodology 51
4. Profile of Budgam and Baramulla Districts 59
5. Findings: Work and Education in Kashmir Society 91
6. Findings: Work Performed by Men and Women in Kashmir Society 105
7. Findings: Health Condition in Kashmir Society 125
8. Findings: Issues Related to Marriage 133
9. Recommendation on Strategy, Policy and Action for Women Emancipation 173
10. Press Reports on National Seminar on Gender Discrimination in Kashmir (1997) 181

List of Members of the Core Group of Experts 207

List of Research Investigators of the Survey 211

Index 213

LIST OF TABLES

Table No.	Title of the Table	Page No.
3.1.	Distribution of Sample in Baramulla District	53
3.2.	Distribution of Sample in Budgam District	54
4.1.	Estimated Population in Jammu and Kashmir State (by District, 1991)	59
4.2.	Area, Density, Rural/Urban, Male/Female Population in Jammu and Kashmir State (districtwise,1981)	61
4.3.	Pattern of Population Growth, 1951-91	62
4.4.	Composition of Male/Female and Rural/ Urban Population, 1981	63
4.5.	Literate/Illiterate Population, 1981	64
4.6.	Religious Composition of Population, 1981	65
4.7.	Number of Villages and Towns, 1971 and 1981	66
4.8.	Number of Working Force by Sex, 1981	68
4.9.	Occupation of Population (sexwise), 1981	69
4.10.	Number of Educational Institutions in Budgam District, 1996	70
4.11.	Number of Educational Institutions in Baramulla District, 1996	71
4.12.	Enrolment of Students in Educational Institutions at Various Levels	73

4.13.	Enrolment of Students in Technical Institutes (subjectwise) in Baramulla District, 1995-97	74
4.14.	Enrolment of Students in Technical Institutes (subjectwise) in Budgam District, 1995-96	75
4.15.	Enrolment of Students in Women's Polytechnic in Budgam District, 1993-96	75
4.16.	Number of Teachers, 1996	76
4.17.	Budgetry Allocation for Education, 1990-94	77
4.18.	Number of Health Centres and Facilities Available Therein, 1996	78
4.19.	Number of Medical Staff, 1998	79
4.20.	Availability of Health Centres and Facilities, 1996	80
4.21.	TRYSEM Beneficiaries, Baramulla District (Last five years)	81
4.22.	PMRY Beneficiaries, Budgam District, (1994-95)	81
4.23.	DWCRA Beneficiaries Budgam District, 1991-94	82
4.24.	DWCRA Beneficiaries, Baramulla District, (1994-96)	83
4.25.	Number of Persons Trained in Handicraft Centres Trades (1988-95)	84
4.26.	Number of Unemployed Persons Registered in District Employment Office, Budgam upto, 1995	85
4.27.	Functioning of Destitute Women's Homes, 1994-95	86
4.28.	Benefits Provided by OAPS, 1995-96	87

4.29.	Vocational Training Centres and Training Courses Provided therein in Baramulla District, 1996	88
4.30.	Vocational Training Centres and Training Courses Provided therein in Budgam District	87
4.31.	OBC/SC-ST Scholarships, District Budgam	89
4.32.	OBC/SC-ST Scholarship Beneficiarier, Baramulla District	89
5.1.	Preference for Girl's Education	92
5.2.	Preference for Boy's Education	94
5.3.	Impact of Education on Marriage Practices	97
5.4.	Different Types of Work Done by Boys and Girls, Baramulla District	100
5.5.	Different Types of Work Done by Boys and Girls, Budgam District	101
5.6.	Age of Marriage for Boys and Girls	103
6.1.	Works Performed by Men and Women	106
6.2.	Activities Performed by Males/Females in Agricultural and Fruit-Growing Fields	108
6.3.	Activities Performed by Males/Females in Agricultural and Fruit-Growing Fields, District Budgam	109
6.4.	Activities Performed by Men and Women in Animal Husbandry, District Baramulla	112
6.5.	Activities Performed by Men and Women in Animal Husbandry, District Budgam	113
6.6.	Should Women Work Outside for Earning Money	114
6.7.	Works done by Women for Earning Money	116
6.8.	Nature of Works Women should do to earn Money	117

6.9.	Control on Assets by Men and Women, (District Baramulla)	119
6.10.	Control on Assets by Men and Women, (District Budgam)	120
6.11.	Decision-making in the Family, (Budgam District)	122
6.12.	Decision-making in the Family, (Baramulla District)	123
7.1.	Number of Children Born in the Family	126
7.2.	Health Facilities Utilized during the Period of Pregnancy	127
7.3.	Number of Abortions of the Women	128
7.4.	Number of Children Survived after Birth	129
7.5.	Medicines used by Women during Pregnancy	130
7.6.	Place of Birth of Children of the Respondents	131
7.7.	Conduct of Delivery of Children	131
8.1.	Payment of Dowry at the time of Marriage of Girls	133
8.2.	Payment of *Mehr* at the time of Divorce	136
8.3.	Incidence of Divorces	137
8.4.	Is it easy for a Husband to Divorce his Wife	138
8.5.	Is it easy for a Wife to get Divorce from her Husband	140
8.6.	Place of Residence of Divorced Women	141
8.7.	Remarriage of Divorcees and Widows	143
8.8.	Remarriage of Men after Divorcees	144
8.9.	Remarriage of Women after Divorce	146
8.10.	Remarriage of Women after Death of their Husbands	147
8.11.	Remarriage of Men after Death of their Wives	148

8.12.	Residence of Widows after Death of their Husbands	150
8.13.	Prevalance of the Practice of Wife-beating	154
8.14.	Inheritance by Women from their Parent's Property	155
8.15.	Amount of Share Women get from their Parent's Property	157
8.16.	Women's Share in their Parent's Property	158
8.17.	Inheritance Rights of Widows	160
8.18.	Approaching the Court for Family Disputes	162
8.19.	Initiative of going to the Court	163
8.20.	Places to which People Migrate to Work during the Winter Months	164
8.21.	Places which the Rural Women visit with and without Male Companion	165

FOREWORD

The role of women in the traditional societies has been characterized by dependency, inferior social status and overall sufferings. In reality they have faced systematic discrimination and institutionalized exploitation at the hands of the male members of these societies. Historical record of the human past reveal clearly that this situation existed more or less in all traditional societies. These propositions about the role and status of women in the past stand as real portraits of the social reality at that time.

A biological division of labour between sexes is part of the scheme of evolution. Men and women are complementary opposites. Each is said to fulfil itself by developing just those qualities lacking in the other. Woman represents love, fidelity, self sacrifice, devotion, tenderness and innocence. Man is thought to represent power, courage, will, strength and labour.

The overall condition of women in general and those in developing countries especially in India in particular, has been far from satisfactory. More than the mere sexual dimorphism, the gender superiority of male has contributed much to the special difficulties that the women face in the sexual division of labour, specific nature of tasks they do at home and outside and even unequal distribution of resources like food within the household which are common features in rural and semi-urban areas where every dawn brings with it a long march in search of fuel, fodder and water. It does not matter if the women are old, young or pregnant. Crucial household needs have to be met day after weary day.

Available studies show that rural women work longer hours than men. This is how one village woman describes her life,

"This is the seventh month of my pregnancy, I am the only adult in the household to take care of my children, two buffaloes, and a calf. My husband is a petty trader in a nearby town. The entire responsibility of the house is on my shoulders. I have to cook, fetch water and provide fodder to animals. In the evening I take them for grazing and collect green fodder. I also have to supervise the ploughing. Where is the time for me to take rest. I usually resume my normal activities just after four to five days after delivery".

The sociological and other studies clearly reveal that women were not considered equal to men in the broader society and were not allowed to become equal and active partners in social life. In many traditional societies, though women participated equally in social, economic and cultural fields, they were secluded, denied important rights such as decision making and control over assets. These views about women were held by men as well as women themselves.

Available information shows that rural women work, for longer hours than men. On an average, women contribute 46 per cent on agriculture, industry and domestic work; men 37 per cent and children 17 per cent. But in domestic activities alone, women contribute half the total human-hours spent and men and children a quarter each. Nearly half the time of the household is spent on basic activities like fetching fuel and water, cooking food and milling grains and a woman on an average has to work for 18 hours a day. A study from the plains of Western UP—an agriculturally prosperous area—shows that even pregnant women spent 14 to 16 hours working in a day. Women's work in the hills and deserts and in arid and semi-arid areas is even harder. The amount of time involving hard, physical labour for the two main activities—collecting fuel and fooder and fetching water—may be as much as 7.2 hours a day.

Despite all this hard labour the traditional practices contribute to women's poor nutritional and health status. Take the case of an individual female born in India or virtually any other developing country. If she survives infancy, the girl will most likely grow up on a diet that does not meet her nutritional requirements. As a child she will work for several hours each day assisting her mother by tending siblings, collecting water and firewood, hurding small animals, weeding the fields or selling wares in the market place. Unlike her brother's task these duties will take precedence over going to school. Consequently she will receive little or no formal education. She will almost inevitably receive insufficient nourishment to compensate for the energy expended in daily chores, not to mention for proper growth and development. Her parents will likely plan to have her married early in her teens. Later in life, as she is taught her main role will be to bear and rear as many children as God brings or her husband desires.

Discrimination in the allocation of food as well as health care and education is a widespread and well documented practice, for example, while strong preferences for male children diminish the value of females, girls are perceived as risky investments in these cultures for a number of reasons including the sizable dowry their parents usually must provide to her prospective husband. She is regarded as "outside wealth" that is handed over to a husband, usually with hefty dowry payments. The deep-rooted bias and prejudice and discrimination against the girl child is the worst kind of gender discrimination.

It is often regarded that the birth of a boy is a boon and that of a girl is a disaster. This has led to female *infanaticide* or amniocentesis. A very recent article on correcting gender bias by Mrs Gouri Sen which appeared in *Hindustan Times* (July 23) points out that according to one estimate more than four million girl children joined the ranks of India's missing women and an estimated 1.2 million lives were snuffed out either through abortion or post-natal murder between 1981 and 1991.

Sex-determination centres using modern foetal testing technology and abortion centres are flourishing and expanding in spite of a Government ban. A couple can always find a doctor willing to take a sonogram or perform amniocentesis and more often than not they abort a female foetus.

Studies from Bangladesh, India, Nepal and Pakistan indicate that boys consistently receive more and better food than their sisters, although the nutritional needs of pre-pubescent boys and girls are virtually identical. A maternal health status report shows that the major contributor to the poor nutritional status of women is "the tradition of feeding men and boys before women and girls, the nutritious foods are served to male members of the family and females would then have left overs."

Moreover, women—having internalized their low status—will feed themselves least in the face of limited food and last in most circumstances. On an average they hardly consume 50-70 per cent of the recommended daily intake of calories. Not surprisingly, anemia is widespread in both pregnant and non-pregnant women. Anaemia—a deficiency in either the quantity or quality of oxygen carrying red blood cells that impedes a woman's ability to resist infection or survive hemorrhage—may result from deficiencies of iron, foliate or vitamin B_{12}. More than half of the pregnant women and 47 per cent of non-pregnant women in developing countries are estimated to suffer from anemia. Anemia increases the risk of dying in child birth by a factor of four and severe anemia is associated with an eight-fold risk of maternal death during pregnancy.

Poor nutrition often worsens later in women's life because of an increasingly heavy workload, the loss of iron stores through menstruation and the combined demands of child bearing. These nutritional defects contribute to what may become lifelong handicaps, such as increasing predisposition to illness, low weight and stunted physical and mental development. Physical immaturity due to stunted growth subsequently leads to far higher rates of pregnancy related problems, including obstructed labour, infections, hemorrhage, ruptured uterus, etc.

Violence against women is another important aspect of gender discrimination and millions of women and girls in every country, on every continent and of every class life under the threat of physical abuse, reports the latest issue entitled "The Progress of Nations" released by the UNICEF, India.

It is estimated that one-third of married women in developing countries are battered by their husbands. This happens even in developed countries. In Germany upto four million women suffer from domestic violence every year. And in India more than 5000 women are killed every year because their dowries are inadequate.

For much of the past two decades, well deserved attention has been paid to the global spread of Human Immuno-Deficiency Virus (HIV) and its deadly consequence AIDS. The focus on AIDS, however, has obscured a more widespread, equally devastating epidemic: Reproductive tract infections. These currently cause far more deaths among women than AIDS does in men and children combined. The rising incidence of both HIV and reproductive tract infections pose grave and unprecedented threats to the lives of women around the world. Millions of women with serious reproductive tract infections suffer in silence. This is partly because many early stage infections often lack obvious symptoms and are not so easily recognized. More importantly, the majority of women live in areas were routine screening for such infections is simply not available. To make matters worse, the women are rarely educated about the prevention of reproductive tract infections. In many cases these are rife with stigmas, taboos and the threat of social ostracism. Fear reinforced by low self-esteem, illiteracy and the fear of violence from or rejection by their partners, prevents millions of women from reporting or discussing any symptoms that might lead to prompt identification and treatment. A number of International Development meetings and forums have begun to reflect in their rhetoric the need for reproductive health care that goes beyond the conventional family planning programme. Nevertheless, the availability of comprehensive services is still more of an exception than a rule. Where they do exist, they are usually provided by non-governmental organizations that can reach only a small share of women in need.

In the absence of a concerted campaign to provide comprehensive reproductive health care, the prognosis for the next generation of women seems to be poor.

Although the biogeography of Kashmir is strikingly different from rest of the country, woman in traditional Kashmiri society has equally shared the sorrows and fortunes of common life. Her function and position has remained distinctly subordinate to man. Although the practice of infanticide, foeticide, dowry deaths were not resorted to, the prejudice against the birth to a female was there. While they enjoyed certain advantages available to Muslim women in traditional environment, they did suffer in many other areas of social life on the other hand. Pt. Prem Nath Bazaz, in his book on Kashmiri women writes:

> "...It is clear that through their long history, Kashmiri women witnessed varying fortunes. At times have risen to pinnacles of glory, distinguished themselves as rulers in their own right, as regents of minor princes, as powerful queens—consort, as diplomats in peace and war, as commanders of armies, as thrifty land-ladies, as builders and reformers, and as perceptors of religious lore... there was no social activity in which they did not participate side by side with their menfolk. Times came when they fell on evil days and were gradually deprived of the rights previously enjoyed by them. However they valiantly struggled against injustice during the long dismal period".

In the traditional Kashmiri society, women generally remained confined to their family household. Their world was confined to their homes. While not considered equal partners in their family life, they were usually subjugated, discriminated and maltreated. In reality, the women in Kashmir were caught in a paradoxical situation.

While their social role was minimal, they participated actively in the economic life, especially among the lower socio-economic groups. In the urban areas, while the women of upper classes/ groups/communities were completely confined to their homes and were not allowed to perform any manual labour outside their homes, women belonging to various occupational groups worked with their men both within and outside their homes for earning a livelihood. But, this active economic role had not given them complete economic independence and higher social status.

However, the change among women in Kashmir started from the early twentieth century, especially from early 1930s, when the freedom movement started here. Two set of factors were responsible for this. Firstly, at the endogenous level, emerging political consciousness, expanding modern education, spread of cultural awareness, deteriorating economic conditions and large-scale social awakening, created a situation in which women felt concerned about their position, especially about their role outside their homes. They started thinking and working about their rights in the broader society. Secondly, at the exogeneous level, there was a strong impact of the outside alien cultural, political and other developments on the people of the valley.

The emancipation of women in Kashmir started with the initiation of a movement for national independence. This movement, in actuality, was responsible for the renaissance of the Kashmiris in general and the Kashmiri women in particular in modern times. Subsequently, in the post-independence decades, while the outside impact continued changing women at ideational and behavioural levels, the economic and educational mobility of women in Kashmir led to the emergence of situation characterized by following three features:

(i) There emerged a mass consciousness among women and men about women's rights in their homes and outside. This had a qualitative impact on the family life, especially in relation to women's role and status;

(ii) The Kashmiri women in general achieved a fair degree of social and cultural mobility which helped in the fast break-down of the institutional structure of the traditional family. Women felt easy to deviate from the traditional practices and enlarge their roles; and

(iii) The Kashmiri women in general developed an interest and motivation to come out of their homes for various purposes like education, employment and entertainment. As a result, many women were accomodated in various employment sectors.

Women have now awakened to the fact that in order to break gender barriers and overcome social bias, women's participation and equality in all developmental processes is essential, as guaranteed in the Constitution.

Article 14 while guaranteeing equality to men and women also empowered the state to adopt measures of positive discrimination in favour of women to assist them to overcome the cumulative socio-economic, educational and political oppression faced by them for centuries.

Article 15 forbids discrimination on grounds of caste, religion, sex, race and place of birth and Article 16 ensures equal opportunities of employment.

As one of the major tools for empowering women, the instrument of education has played a significant role. It has shifted their traditional role as housewives and mothers to non-traditional roles as producers, partners and partakers in national development. Although India still has the distinction of having the largest number of illiterate women, the female literacy rate has gone up from 0.60 per cent in 1901 to 39.29 per cent in 1991 and the male-female gender gap in literacy is narrowing down. In higher education only 12 per cent of the total enrolment of women was recorded in 1950-51, but during 1993-94, this touched a figure of 32.2 per cent in the Universities.

Women's economic empowerment is increasing—in 1971, the net participation rate was 14.2 per cent and in 1991, it reached 22.3 per cent. The share in organised sector has increased to 14 per cent in 1991. Women in Government service account for 13.6 per cent, but in administrative services their share is 7-10 per cent. However, there are only 9 or 10 women Vice-Chancellor's out of 228.

Several Acts and other social legislations like Hindu Marriage Act, Dowry Act, Maternity Benefit Act, Termination of Pregnancy Act, Child Marriage Restraint Act, Hindu Succession

Act and Immoral Traffic Act have been enacted from time to time during the past 50 years to remove gender discrimination and enhance empowerment of women.

Major Initiatives for Women's Empowerment

During the recent years, a number of major initiatives have been taken for empowerment of women.

1. *Setting up of Rashtriya Mahila Kosh:* A National credit fund for women set up in 1993, to empower poor and assetless women through extended credit and thrift;

2. *Mahila Samridhi Yojna:* Set up in 1993, to promote the habit of saving, with incentives from Government.

3. *Indira Mahila Yojna:* Launched in 1995, it aims at integrated development of women through convergence of all sectoral programmes through a nodal agency at the village level.

4. *Panchayat Raj Act, 1993:* A very revolutionary concept in recognising women's contribution to local self government at grassroot level giving 30 per cent representation to women in Village Panchayats, Panchayat Samitis, and Zila Parishads. Today we have nearly seven lakh women Panches, Sarpanches and Chairpersons of Panchayat bodies in the areas of local government with women thus, participating in political and administrative processes.

Women have also been given their due share in several rural development programmes—IRDP, JRY, TRYSEM, etc.

The year 1995, was a milestone in the Women's Movement which witnessed the struggle of women around the world and in India, as they prepared for the Beijing Fourth World Conference on Women. The covenant arrived at Beijing by women and men of the world may well represent our hopes for the future. The Declaration and Platform for action adopted, to which India is signatory, among other things, clearly states that the Government is:

(a) Determined to advance the goals of equality, development of peace for all women everywhere in the interest of all humanity;

(b) Recognizes that the status of women has advanced in some important respects in the past decade, but that progress has been uneven, inequalities between women and men have persisted and major obstacles remain, with serious consequences for the well being of all people; and

(c) That we dedicate ourselves unreservedly to addressing these constraints and obstacles, thus, enhancing further the advancement and empowerment of all women all over the world and agree that this requires urgent action in the spirit of determination, hope, cooperation and solidarity, now to carry us forward into the next century.

The crusade against gender discrimination is on and looking back through the 50 years of India's Independence, a reasonable degree of empowerment of women attained, the male-female gap has been considerably reduced and if this much could be achieved in just 50 years without any greater participation of women and so many acts, guarantees and programmes, I am sure much more would be achieved in the next decade and after. Only the women must realise that they have constitutional rights for equality, they must come forward, shun the age old beliefs, dogmas, superstitions and also the much abused cruel attitude of mother-in-law treatment, against which the famous Lala Arifa of Kashmir is on record.

The present study is, in fact, addressed to these differences. The basis are the findings on gender discrimination in the two important districts of Kashmir—Budgam and Baramulla. Most important areas of discrimination have been highlighted and I hope the study shall further debate on important themes and work out possible strategies for follow up action and also suggest ways to help the desperate women in Kashmir.

Professor M.Y. Qadri
Vice-Chancellor
University of Kashmir,
Srinagar

PREFACE

We can define women's rights as a guarantee of political, social and economic equality for women in a society that traditionally confers more status and freedom to men. Among these rights are control of property, equality of opportunity in education and employment, suffrage and sexual freedom. The women's rights movement, also known as feminism and women's liberation, arose in Europe in the late 18th century. Although, by 1970, most women throughout the world had gained many rights according to law, in fact, complete economic and social equality with men remained to be achieved.

In most traditional societies, women generally were at a disadvantage. Their education was limited to learning domestic skills and they had no access to positions of power. Marriage was almost a necessity as a means of support or protection. Pressure was constant to produce many children. A married woman usually took her husband's status and lived with his family, with little recourse in case of ill-treatment or non-support.

Some exceptions to women's dependence on men did exist. In ancient Babylonia and Egypt, women had property rights and in medieval Europe they could join craft guilds. Some women had religious authority, for example, as Siberian shamans and Roman priestesses. Occasionally, women had political authority such as Egyptian and Byzantine queens, heads of medieval nunneries and Iroquois women, who appointed men to clan and tribal councils. A few highly cultivated women flourished in ancient Rome, China and Renaissance Europe.

Men of the lower classes also lacked rights, but they could console themselves by feeling superior to women. Struggling to preserve their dignity in a harsh world, such men were unlikely to sympathize with the plight of women.

The age of enlightenment, with its egalitarian political emphasis, and the industrial revolution, which caused economic and social causes, provided a favourable climate for the rise of feminism, along with other reform movements in the late 18th and 19th centuries. In France, during the French Revolution, women's republican clubs pleaded that the goals of liberty, equality and fraternity should apply to all regardless of sex. But, the subsequent adoption of the Code Napoleon, based on Roman Law, obliterated any immediate realization of such hopes on the continent. In England, Mary Wollstonecraft wrote a Vindication of the Rights of Women (1972), the first major modern feminist work. Its demands for equality and its revolutionary tone made it unacceptable at that time.

Of deeper significance for women was the Industrial Revolution. The transformation of handicrafts, which women had always carried on at home without pay, into machine-powered mass production meant that lower class women could become wage earners in factories. This was the beginning of their independence, although factory conditions were hazardous and their pay, lower than men's, was legally controlled by their husbands. At the same time, middle and upper class women were expected to stay at home as idle, decorative symbols of their husbands' economic success. The only other option for respectable women of any class was to work as governesses, clerks, shop assistants and servants. Such conditions encouraged the feminist movement.

The women's rights movement has made some progress. In more than 90 per cent of the nations, women can vote and hold public office. Aided by the United Nations Commission on the Status of Women (1946), women in many nations have gained legal rights and fuller access to education and all professions. However, the advent of industrialization in non-western nations has destroyed some traditional economic arrangements that favoured women and has made underpaid factory labour the only work available to them. In 1975, the UN launched a Decade for Women Programme and major conferences were held in 1975, 1980 and 1985.

Discrimination is any situation in which a group or individual is treated differently based on something other than individual reason, usually their membership in a socially distinct group or category. Such categories would include ethnicity, sex, religion, age or disability. Discrimination can be viewed as favourable or unfavourable, depending on whether a person receives favours or opportunities or is denied of them. In modern usage, "discrimination" is usually considered unfavourable. Women have historically been victimized by discrimination in voting, inheritance, employment and other civil rights. Kashmir is a traditional society with a rich heritage. Numerous women scholars have shown light to the society during the past.

In August 1995, a seminar on the 'status of women' was organised at Budgam. It was attended by the prominent women activists/officials of the state and SAHELI, New Delhi. The seminar was presided over by Dr. Jon E. Rohde, Chief, India Country Office, UNICEF, New Delhi. In this seminar, it was felt that a study on status of discrimination in Kashmir Valley should be undertaken. The aim of the study was to derive ground/ empirical knowledge about the status of women, which will help the planners in removing the unfavourable discrimination through policy intervention.

Later on, detailed discussions took place with Mr. U. Ghosh, ACS (Agri.), M.M. Bhat (Director, Rural Development, Kashmir), Prof. M.I. Parry (IMPA) and Dr. R.K. Rath and UNICEF regarding the modality of the study. It was felt that two districts should be taken for the study. Budgam was selected because of its indicator of backwardness and Baramulla for its proximity to border and indicators of less backwardness in the valley.

Phase I of the study comprising of field visits, interviews, etc., was conducted by Ms. Kalpana Mehta and Maitreya Ghatak, experts to UNFPA in similar study in Haryana state in November 1995. The outcome of phase I was preparation and finalization of questionnaires and recommendation for micro studies.

Phase II of the study involved very detailed interviews, field visits by scholars and students of Department of Sociology, University of Kashmir, Srinagar in Aparil-May 1996 and submission of the final report. This phase was completed under overall guidance of Dr. Bashir Ahmad Dabla (Head, Department of Sociology, Kashmir University). S. Khurshidul Islam was the field supervisor for this phase. They held series of discussions with the Gender Study Group of District Red Cross Society, Budgam headed by Sandeep K. Nayak, Deputy Commissioner and with district officers viz. A.R. Khan (Assistant Commissioner, development), Dr. Manzoor Hussain (Chief Medical Officer), Mrs. Hamida Shah (Chief Education Officer), Mrs. Mehmooda (D.E.P.O.), Mr. M.D. Handoo (District Social Welfare Officer), Mrs. Ezabir Ali, A.P.O. (DWCRA), Abdul Aziz Sofi (Chief Planning Officer) and Sajjad Hussain (Information Officer) before finalization of the report.

I feel extremely grateful to Mr. A.R. Rather (Hon'ble Agriculture Minister) and Mr. H.H. Taibji (Financial Commissioner, Agriculture and Rural Development) for encouraging this type of work in Jammu and Kashmir state, which has not been carried out so far.

It is hoped that this unique study conducted in the valley during very difficult times will help the policy makers.

Srinagar

Sundeep K. Nayak I.A.S.
Development Commissioner
District Srinagar
Jammu and Kashmir State

1

INTRODUCTION

Women in the Global Context

The sociological investigation of the human society at the global level has that women in general in the distant and recent past faced unfair and unequal treatment at the hands of their own and other men. Their role in totality was characterized with dependency, inferiority and acute suffering. They lived like somebody's property. In actuality, they have faced systematic discrimination institutionalized suppression and multi-dimensional exploitation. The historical records of the human past reveals that this situation related to women prevailed more or less in all human societies situated in all continents. This situation also prevailed irrespective of human societies situated in all continents. This situation also prevailed irrespective of human societies' differences in race, region, religion, economy, social structure, culture, and in other fields of life. These sociological propositions about the status and role of women in the traditional societies are not mere theoretical or ideological abstractions, but essentially stand for the empirical and realistic social reality of the human past. It may be argued that while some human societies practised highest degree of negative attitude and behaviour towards women, other societies had adopted lowest degree in this regard.

However, the fact of contemporary importance stands that women at the global level and in continuity have undergone wider and deeper processes of transformation in the earlier and current centuries. While women in the European and American continents have undergone radical transformation in the previous few centuries, women in the Asian, African and Latin American continents faced certain degree of change in the present century. This multifarious change among women in the developed as well as developing countries had complete or partial effect on the traditional status and role of women in these societies. This large-scale, deep-rooted and multifaceted change among women can primarily be related to the short-term and long-term implications of the processes of modernization, especially development and change. While change refers to the processes of industrialization, urbanization, demographic transformation, secularization, adoption of science and technology in day-to-day life, scientific temper, modern education, materialistic worldview and so on, development points toward improvement in overall conditions of life, especially increase in income, literacy, exposure, improvement in health-nutrition and total advancement in personality and societal traits.

It was in the context of preceding social dynamics that women started undergoing basic change and consequently developing new role and status for themselves as well as for the entire womenfolk. The conditions of women in India must essentially be seen in this background.

Women in India

Like the women in other Asian and African societies, women in India in the past were trapped in a traditional situation which was characterized by discrimination, suppression, inequality and other similar features. The Hindu caste system and its implications had made the condition of women worse and they were not allowed to challenge the then existing situation. However, the change among women here could neither be stopped nor resisted. Consequently, women in the broader Indian society underwent significant degree of change in many fields of life, especially education, employment, health and nutrition.

This process of women's emancipation in India was accelerated in the post-independence era. The governments in India, irrespective of their political and ideological differences, pursued the grand objective of women's betterment in totality. This objective was made an important part of the national planning and development processes. Successive development plans, at the central as well as at the state level, initiated several programmes and schemes for women's betterment.

On the other hand, many voluntary agencies and organizations, which emerged in India in the recent decades, played a significant and effective role in the overall betterment of women here. They worked constantly and systematically to improve general conditions of women in rural and urban India. It has been observed that these NGOs efforts have proved highly useful in individual and group cases. They proved more successful because of women's confidence in them and their acceptability among women.

As a result of serious efforts on the part of GOs and NGOs in the post-independence period, the conditions of women in every part/region of India have improved significantly, though not satisfactorily. This present situation is characterized with three main feature.

Features of Change

First, the change in the position of Indian women has penetrated all communities, groups and regions. The view upheld by some that women of some communities/groups/ regions have not been touched by the general improvement in the status is not correct. In actuality, women of all communities in India have responded positively to the processes of change in varying degrees. This change may be lesser quantitatively, but it stands significant in the relative context. The sociological investigations of women in many parts/states of India, belonging to the minority community of Muslims, have revealed that they have accepted and adopted change in their attitudes and behaviour. In some fields, they have marched ahead of the women of other communities in India. A study carried out in the Kashmir valley by Dr. Bashir Ahmad Dabla on the theme of 'Working Women in Kashmir' provides more than sufficient evidence on the crucial changes which the Muslim women in

Kashmir have accepted, adopted (in their life patterns) and propagate (for the next generation).

Second, change among women in India has to be seen in a contextual form. It implies that this change is neither consistent nor logical completely. There has not emerged inevitable relationship between change in one field of life and the other. For example, no necessary correspondence has developed between changes at the ideational and behavioural levels among women. Other studies have revealed that women had undergone a considerable degree of mobility in the economic field, but it was not followed, correspondingly and necessarily, by mobility in the social and other fields.

Third, women belonging to varying groups and classes and different communities have not responded to the processes of change in the same way, interest, vigour and intensity. Sociologically speaking, that situation was not expected too. As is the case with natural dynamics, different ethnic, religious and regional groups have responded to the processes of change differently.

Women in Kashmir

In the traditional Kashmiri society, women generally remained confined to or around the family. Their world of activities was confined within the borders of their patrilocal household. While not considered equal inside as well as outside their families, they were usually subjugated, abused, discriminated and maltreated in the social life. They could not develop their individual personality or be independent from the males. Actually, they remained dependent on their males throughout their lives. As daughters, they remained dependent on fathers/male guardians; as wives, on their husbands; and as mothers, on their sons. This lifecycle of female dependency was supported by the culture and religion. This dependence was so deeprooted that even the personal matters of women in the family were decided by the eldest male member/s. Their income was usually considered the family's income and was often received as well spent by the males. It is important to note here that majority of women in the valley were economically productive mainly due to the nature of economic activities here. Most of traditional economic sectors/fields were directly or indirectly related to the world-famous Kashmiri handicrafts. The women here in rural and urban areas composed the major part of workers in these sectors/fields. It is estimated that more than 50 per cent of workers in the handicraft sector/fields are women.

The complete domination of men over women crudely reflected in the maltreatment which the latter got at the hands of the former. The women, especially wives, were beaten in some families and there was no collective protest against this brutal practice. Though, some individual protests were observed, but these were insignificant and ineffective. Consequently, the practice of wife-beating was considered an 'undesirable normal practice' in the family context. Moreover, the women in large numbers were not allowed even to participate in the decision-making process. In actuality, all important decisions related to all matters, including decisions about women, were the exclusive prerogative of elder members of the family. Women were allowed even to participate in the deliberations regarding decisions.

Women in the traditional Kashmiri society were considered unequal, inferior and weak (mentally and physically). These notions were supported by myths, dogmas and traditional belief systems. Many women too believed strongly in these men-created notions and ideas, which had a strong impact on the behaviour of women in the entire life. However, strict adherence to the practice of endogamy kept the women here in close contact with their parental/paternal families. This type of relationship between families put a serious restraint on bad treatment of women at the hands of their husbands and their families.

Though Islam allowed the practice of polygamy with certain conditions and limitations, it was never common among the Muslims in Kashmir. The practice was socially insignificant and was generally considered 'undesirable' because of its abuse by some individuals. Moreover, factors like meagre income, underlying feeling that justice cannot be done to two or more wives at a time, and the constant tension in the family reduced further the occurrence of polygamy. The general argument presented was that if you cannot do justice to more than one wife, you should/must not marry second/third/fourth woman. No statistical figures are available about the number of polygamous marriages in the valley. However, experts in Kashmir feel that its number is very less. While three or four wives type of marriages were non-existent, two wives type of marriage had some occurrence. The latter type of marriage was done because of the death or ill-health of the first wife or her insterility.

Similarly, the practice of divorce, religiously allowed with certain obligation on the part of the husband, was not common in the valley. No official or unofficial figures are available in this regard. The concerned experts here feel that divorces were rare in the valley and this number was socially neglible. This situation may be explained by factors like close relations between families, fear of retaliation of divorce from the other side, and strong social pressure against divorce.

The Islamic *shariah* allowed the Muslim women to inherit a particular share from the property of their parents and husbands. Though, these inheritance rights for women in the valley existed in theory, these were denied to them in practice. In actuality, a customary law was developed which did not allow a due share to women from their parental property. Again, though, the *mehr* stood as a legal right (the payment of which must be made before the finalization of marriage), it was usually denied to them in part or full in practice.

In reality, the women in Kashmir in the past were caught in a paradoxical situation. While their social role was projected as minimal, they participated actively in social, economic and other activities. In urban areas, while the women of *sayyid* and *hojja* families were confined completely to their homes and were not allowed to perform any manual labour outside their homes, women belonging to various occupational groups/communities worked with their men both within and outside their homes for earning sufficient amount of money required to fulfil the family needs. In the rural areas, all women worked side by side with their family members in the agricultural fields.

The women in Kashmir generally did not practise purdah which meant the wearing of the formal *burqa* from head to toe. This practice applied to all groups of the Kashmiri society except the *sayyid* and *hojja* women. These two groups practised various forms of purdah due to religious and social reasons.

Generally, there prevailed no segregation between women and men in the traditional society in Kashmir. The interaction between the opposite sexes usually took place at all levels, in all fields and in all sections of society. In fact, the institutional arrangement in the occupations in the valley was developed in such a way that the male-female interaction, both with insiders and outsiders, seemed a must.

Change among Women in Kashmir

The situation of women explained above prevailed for centuries in the Kashmir valley and has been recorded by some historians, missionaries, tourists and travellers. It is generally believed by the experts that conditions in Kashmir in general and the Kashmiri women in particular started undergoing change from the early decades of the 20th century. Two major sets of factors are mainly responsible for the initiation of this broader and deeper change. First, at the endogenous level, emerging political consciousness, expanding modern education, spreading of cultural awareness, deteriorating economic conditions and large-scale social awakening created a situation in which women felt concerned about their position. They also started thinking about their rights in the broader social contact. Second, at the exogenous level, there was a strong impact of the process of *neubremization* which refers to a process of impact of the outside developments on the inhabitants in the valley. Accordingly, all political, social, economic and other developments in the Indian subcontinent, especially erstwhile united Panjab and Delhi, had necessary impact on overall situation in the Kashmir valley. Interaction with and exposure to the outsiders/aliens made adoption of change easy, contextual and relevant.

Mass change among women in Kashmir started from early twentieth century, especially from early 1930s, when the freedom movement started in the state. The women in the valley in general participated in that movement against the feudal rule of the Maharaja dynasty in large numbers and their men put no restriction on them. That was the first time in Kashmir history when women in large numbers came out of their homes and participated in a social-political movement. It was essentially in the context of that movement that women in Kashmir (and in the state of Jammu and Kashmir at large) were provided equal rights (to men's rights) which were enshrined in the Naya Kashmir Programme in 1983, that guided all post-independence period governments in Jammu and Kashmir state. In that changing context, while the *sayyid-hojja* women responded early and fully to the changing processes, other women, belonging to lower socio-economic groups/classes responded to change very late.

After 1947, when the local political leadership assumed political power, successive governments in Jammu and Kashmir state, irrespective of political and ideological differences, attempted to improve the conditions of women here. Many efforts in this direction were started. Free education, including technical and professional education, was provided to the women from primary to the university level. Women were assured jobs in government offices, technical-professional institutes, public and private enterprises and commercial-business establishments. The government also safeguarded political, economic and social rights of women. However, it was observed that these programmes for women's welfare were neither properly planned nor carried out with commitment and seriousness. The political instability in the state in the entire post-1947 period was mainly responsible for this situation.

Post-independence Developments Related to Women

In the post-independence decades in Jammu and Kashmir state, three major developments related to women took place. These developments were:

Firstly, there emerged a mass consciousness among women (and other members of society too) about their rights within as well as outside their homes. This had a qualitative impact on the family life, especially in relation to the status and role of women;

Secondly, the Kashmiri women in general and belonging to all classes, groups and communities achieved at fair degree of social and cultural mobility, which also helped in the fast breakdown of the institutional structure of the traditional family. In this situational context, women felt relatively easy to deviate from the traditional practices and enlarge their role.

Thirdly, most important, the Kashmiri women at large developed motivation and interest in coming out of their homes for various purposes like education, employment and entertainment. As a result of this development, many women were recruited in various employment sectors. In actuality, there emerged a general pattern in rural as well as urban areas according to which all educated girls sought education, and subsequently, employment necessarily.

It is important to note here that the above-mentioned changes among women were directed towards their change and development. In totality, these changes contribute step-by-step to their emancipation. However, these changes were associated with other problems for womens and their family members. Prominent among these problems include problems of child bearing and child rearing, their undesirable socialization and uncontrolled behaviour, women's dual role and post-marital conflict/maladjustment, and their discrimination and harassment in out-home situations. It follows that women in the traditional Kashmiri society faced one set of problems such as total dependence on men, lower social status, confining their role to their homes, imposition of ideas and behaviour related to the women. Now, in the changing situation, women faced another set of problems which included women's dual role, child bearing and child rearing problems, and marital disharmony. In this situation, the women's problems became complex and their complexity has been increasing day by day. Moreover, the short-term and long-term implications of these problems are completely undesirable for women and the society at large.

Problems of Women

The problems of women in the Kashmir valley are multifarious and are felt in every field of life. However, we have identified five primary and crucial problems of women, the details of which follow:

Social Problems

- practice of dowry
- non-payment of *mahr*
- status of wife
- practice of polygamy
- divorce to women
- remarriage of divorcees and widows
- denial of women's share in the parental property
- post-marital relations
- practice of wife-beating
- undesirable places of work
- dual role of working women
- problems of childcare
- undesirable socialization of children
- family disorganization and its implications.

Economic Problems

- pattern of traditional occupations and women's participation
- occupational mobility and women
- women's work on agricultural land
- payment of wages to women workers
- women workers in the handicraft sector
- exploitation of women workers
- women's work outside their homes
- regular salary and economic independence of women
- pattern of spending by working women

- economic activities performed by women
- educated women and government jobs
- women benefited by governmental programmes.

Educational Problems

- literacy among women
- educated persons in the families of parents and husbands
- availability of educational facilities
- school-going children in the family
- dropouts from the school
- cost of education of children
- career-oriented education for women.

Health Problems

- health institutions and facilities available
- immunization of children
- common diseases among children and their mothers
- pre-natal and post-natal care
- conduct and place of delivery
- number of children of women
- effects of having more children
- response to the illness by women
- visit to the local P.H.C.
- breast feeding of children
- awareness about family planning.

Discrimination Problems

- harassment of working women
- discrimination in the wage payment
- complaint against lesser wages
- discrimination of women in handicraft sector
- discrimination of women in inheritance rights

- religion and discrimination against women
- laws against women's interests
- authority pattern of women
- discrimination against girl child
- abortion of female foetus by women.

It is in the above thematic framework that we have focussed on the women in Kashmir to know their multidimensional problems. As the existing situation reveals, these dimensions of women's problems represent their basic, crucial and central problems. In actuality, these various problems portray the totality of women's problems.

2

WOMEN AND SOCIETY : VIEWS ABOUT GENDER DISCRIMINATION

Meaning and Scope

In general, the term 'gender' refers to the distinction between males and females according to anatomical sex. In the sociological usage, it refers to a social division usually based on anatomical sex. According to Ann Oakley, who introduced the term in the field of sociology, while sex refers to the biological division in to male and female, gender essentially means the parallel and socially unequal division into femininity and masculinity. So, the gender draws attention primarily to the socially constructed aspects of differences between men and women. Sociologists and social psychologists argue that while sex refers to the biological characteristics by which human beings are categorized as male or female, gender conveys the social and psychological attributes by which human beings are categorized as masculine or feminine. Sociologists, again, stress that, within the sociological discourse, gender should be used when refering to the socially-created division of society into those who are masculine and those who are feminine.

In actuality, the term 'gender' has been extended to refer not only the individual identity and personality, but, also at the symbolic level, to cultural ideals and stereotypes of masculinity and feminity. At the structural level, it refers to the sexual division of labour in institutions and organizations. In this thermotic context, social factors such as class, age, race, religion and ethnicity shape the meaning, expression and experience of 'gender'. Thus, it essentially points towards the social phenomenon, rooted in particular ideology/values, which reflects in different and unequal behaviour-pattern of males and females that determines the nature of discrimination against the latter.

The conception of 'gender discrimination' can be further clarified by comparing it with other terms. The 'gender differentiation' points to the process in which biological differences between males and females are assigned social significance and are used as a means of social classification.

The 'gender stratification' refers to any process by which the gender becomes the basis of social stratification, in which the perceived differences between the genders become ranked and evaluated in a systematic way. The 'gender segregation' conveys the ideas related to the unequal distribution of men and women in the occupational structure.

Repercussion of Gender Discrimination

After studying different societies in the world, sociologists have held that the practice of gender discrimination at the global level has generally led to:

(a) women being ascribed specific feminine roles and a gender identity through the processes of socialization;

(b) women being secluded from public activities in industrial societies by relegating their activities to the private dornain of the home;

(c) women being allocated inferior and degrading activities; and

(d) women being subjected to stereotypical ideologies which define women as weak and emotionally dependent on men.

The phenomenon of 'gender discrimination' stands at the global level, in all societies of the world irrespective of their differences in region, religion, economy, polity, culture, education, social structure and language. However, it has been observed that while the practice of gender discrimination is relatively low in the developed societies, the degree of discrimination in the developing societies is relatively high. This reveals certain degree of co-relation between the degree of gender discrimination and the level of development.

Image of Women in Cross-Cultural Societies

The sociological studies in cross-cultural societies have revealed that women were not considered equal to men at the social level and were not allowed to become active partners in the social life. In some traditional societies, though women participated equally in social and cultural fields and were economically productive, they were secluded, denied important rights and suppressed forcefully. These studies reveal the views about the women held by men and women themselves. These views include the following:

> women produce children; women are mothers and wives only; they do the cooking, mending, sewing and washing; they take care of men and are subordinate to the male authority; they have to be excluded from high status occupations and positions of power.

Various Views about Gender Discrimination

The theme of the relationship between women and society, with special focus on gender differentiation/discrimination, has been dealt by numerous sociologists and other social scientists in the previous few decades in the West. Here our attempt is to present briefly the prominent views about women and society.

Though, there is disagreement about the exact nature and consequences of the biological difference between women and men, some sociologists, anthropologists and psychologists argue that it is sufficient to explain the basic sexual division of labour in human societies.

Lionel Tiger and Robin Fox

These anthropologists argue that men are more aggressive and dominant than women. These features are usually genetically based. These differences are partly due to genetic inheritance from man's primate ancestors and partly due to a genetic adaptation to a hunting way of life. Males hunt which is an aggressive activity. They protect the band and fight with other bands. Thus, they develop the positions of power, especially in relation to women. Tiger and Fox see the men's dominance as a sex-related characteristic, politics stands primarily as the province of men in the Australian Aborigine and in the House of Commons and House of Lords.

In the preceding context, these anthropologists further say that male and female biogrammars are adapted to a sexual division of labour in a primitive society. Compared to cultural change, genetic change is not fast. Thus, the male and female biogrammars of a hunting existence continue in modern/industrial society. It follows that attempts to abolish the particular gender roles and replace them with unisex roles, according to these anthropologists, will go against the natural order.

G.P. Murdock

Murdock upholds the view that the biological differences, such as the greater physical strength of men and that women bear children determine the gender roles. Given the biological differences between men and women, a sexual division of labour seems the efficient way of developing social order.

In a cross-cultural survey of more than two hundred societies, which ranged from hunting-gathering bands to modern nation states, he found the following tasks for different sexes:

Men : hunting, lumbering, mining;

Women : cooking, gathering vegetable products, water carrying and making clothes.

Not handicapped, like the women by the physiological burdens of pregnancy and nursing, man can range farther afield to hunt, to fish and to trade. On the other hand, woman, because of biological function of child bearing and nursing, is tied to the home base. Finally, Murdock concludes that "the advantages inherent in a division of labour by sex presumably account for its universality."

Talcott Parsons

According to T. Parsons, the biological differences between the sexes provide the foundation for the sexual division of labour in the industrial society. He characterizes the women's role in the family as expressive which means she provides warmth, security and emotional support. This is essential for effective socialization of the young. It is only a short step from applying these qualities to her children to applying them also to her husband, which stands as the second function of the nuclear family.

The male breadwinner spends his working day competing in an achievement oriented society. This instrumental role leads to stress and anxiety. The expressive female role relieves this tension with her love, consideration and understanding.

Finally, Murdock argued that for the nuclear family to operate efficiently as a social system, there must be a clear-cut and relevant division of labour. In a way, "the instrumental and expressive role (of family) complement each other. Like button and a buttonhole."

John Bowlby

Bowlby examines the role of women in the psychological perspective. He puts forward the argument that a mother's place is in the home,caring for children especially during their earlier years. He says that it is essential for mental health that the infant and young child should experience a warm, intimate continuous relationship with the mother.

Bowlby's arguments imply that there is a genetically based psychological need for a close and intimate mother-child relationship. In this context, the role of mother is firmly and closely related to the female.

Ann Oakley

Oakley, a sociologist, takes a strong position which says that:

> "not only is the division of labour by sex not universal, but there is no reason why it should be. Human cultures are diverse and endlessly variable."

She says that Murdock's own data negates the assumption that biology solely determines the social division of labour. On the basis of numerous studies by Oakley, she maintains that biology appears to have little or no influence on women's roles. In these societies, while the roles of father and mother are not sharply differentiated, both sexes share responsibility for the care of children.

Oakley also refutes the arguments put forward by Parsons by saying that, in the Kibbutze situation, the system other than the family and the female-mother role can effectively socialize the young. She also argues that the expressive housewife-mother role is not necessary for the functioning of the family unit. It merely exists for the convenience of men.

Oakley concludes that:

> gender roles are culturally rather than biologically determined. Evidence from a number of different societies shows that there are no tasks (apart from child rearing) which are performed exclusively by females. Biological characteristics do not bar women from particular occupations. The mother role is a cultural construction. Evidence from several societies indicates that children do not require a close, intimate and continuous relationship with a female mother figure.

Bruno Bettelheim

Bettelheim, a psychiatrist and specialized in child development, presents the view that a close, continuous mother-child relationship is not essential for effective socialization. Compared to Western society, there is a strong pressure to conform to group norms and as a result, he found that children tend to be less individualistic. In most of the cases, they develop a collective rather than personal sense of self. Bettelheim further said that. In the Israeli Kibutz context, parents expect little intimacy with their children and do not hope for or wish for a one-to-one relationship with them.

On the basis of his study of the Israeli Kibutz, Bettelheim concluded that:

> Children raised by educators in group homes can and do fare a lot better than many children raised by their mothers in poverty-striken homes, and better than quite a few raised at home by their middle-class parents.

Ernestine Friedl

Friedl, an anthropologist, provides an explanation for the sexual division of labour and male dominance. She supports a cultural explanation, noting that there exist great variations in gender roles between societies. In this connection, she observes that in some societies, activities such as weaving, pottery making and tailoring are thought to be 'naturally men's' tasks, in others, women's. At the same time, in societies where such tasks are defined as male roles, they carry higher prestige than in societies where they are assigned to women.

Friedl sees this situation as a reflection of male dominance which, according to her, refers to a situation in which men have highly preferential access to those activities to which society accords the greatest value and the exercise of which permits a measure of control over others. She maintains that this situation exists more or less in all societies despite their differences.

Friedl argues that the degree of male dominance is:

> a consequence of the frequency with which men have greater rights than women to distribute goods outside the domestic group.

It follows that men are dominant because they control the exchange of valued goods beyond the family group. This activity necessarily brings prestige and power to men than to women. It also follows that the greater their control over valued goods outside the family, the greater the dominance of men over women.

Friedl also presents biological arguments in order to explain the sexual division of labour. She says that women are primarily responsible for cultivation, men for clearing and defending the land and exchanging goods with other groups. She also maintains that "a population can survive the loss of men more easily than that of women." The loss of women will reduce the potential size of the population, the loss of men will not necessarily do so, since one man can impregnate many women.

Sherry B. Ortner

Ortner provides a general explanation for the phenomenon of the "universal devaluation of women". She maintains that it is not biology as such that ascribes women to their status in society, but the way in which every culture defines and evaluates female biology. It follows that if this universal evaluation changed, then the basis for female subordination would be removed.

The universal evaluation of culture as superior to nature is the basic reason for the devaluation of women. Women, according to Ortner, are seen closer to nature than men and therefore as inferior to men at the global level. Her argument goes on the following lines:

> Women are universally defined as closer to nature because their bodies physiological functions are more concerned with the natural processes surrounding the reproduction of species, which (processes) include menstruation, pregnancy, childbirth and lactation. They are also responsible for socialization of infants and young. Women's closest relationship with their children make them and family closer to nature. Further, the 'woman's psyche' is considered very close to nature.

On the other hand, men, in comparison, are engaged in politics, warfare and religion and have wider contacts. Men are also seen as more objective, less emotional, and more abstract in thought process.

Ortner concludes that since culture is seen as superior to nature, women's psyche is devalued and men come out on top. Moreover, in terms of her biology, physiological processes, social roles and psychology. woman appears as something intermediate between culture and nature.

Mary K. Benet

In the context of the industrial revolution in the West, the role and status of women (with special reference to gender differenciation/discrimination) faced a new situation that led to their partial or complete change. The prominent views in this background were presented by many social scientists and are as follows:

Benet presented the view that women's jobs are often extentions of their domestic role which involves carring for, waiting on, serving, clearing and tidying up after others. Thus, the secretary also acts as wife, mother and so on. She argues that office work is the business equivalent of housekeeping since both jobs are custodial, concerned with tidying up, putting away and restoring order rather than producing anything. The analogy between housework and paid employment can even be extended to professions such as school-teaching.

The fact that women tend to the employed in 'women jobs' means that measures such as equal pay will not significantly affect their market situation. Equality with men in the labour market requires either an abolition of sexual division of labour or an upgrading of women's jobs. Benet felt that the first alternative would involve men and women being represented at all grades in all occupations in proportions to their numbers in the labour force. The second alternative would involve raising the pay and status of women's jobs to a level where they fall within the same range of pay and status differentials as men's jobs.

Theodore Caplow

Caplow explains the following reasons for the relegation of women to the bottom of the occupational structure:

Firstly, the primary status of women is determined as mothers and housewives. As such, their careers are discontinuous. It is because they move out of the labour market to produce and rear children.

Secondly, women are secondary breadwinners compared to the male family head. This encourages the attitude that it is right and proper that women should be paid less than men.

Thirdly, due to mother-housewife role, women are less geographically mobile than men. The family is much more likely to move house to follow the husband's career than that of the wife. This helps to explain the link between women and low status, jobs, since a successful career often requires residential mobility.

Fourthly, there is a large reserve of employable women, which usually means that the demand for work will exceed its supply. As a result, employees will not to have to attract female labour with high wages, career opportunities and improved working conditions.

Finally, there is a vast array of rules and statutes dealing with the employment of women. These regulations limit their hours of work and bar them from many occupations, particularly the more strenuous.

Caplow argues that the market situation of women is further influenced by two themes of the American culture. First, except in family relationships, males should not be directly subordinate to females. Second, except in family and sexual relationships, intimate groups should be composed of either sex, but never both. These themes are expressed in the occupational sphere in the following way. Men generally occupy positions of authority and work groups are usually single sexed. From single sexed work groups, it is only a short step to the sexual division of labour and the idea of 'men's work' and 'women's work' in the job market.

Frank Parkin

Parkin puts forward the assumption (in the fast industrial context) that the family and not the individual is the basic unit of analysis in the class system. He thinks on the lines that the social and economic rewards of women are largely determined by their marital and family relationships and in particular, by the status of the male breadwinner. He states that:

> If the wives and daughters of unskilled labourers have some things in common with the wives and daughters of wealthy landowners, there can be no doubt that the differences in their overall situation are far more striking and significant.

In other words, the inequalities of sexual status are insignificant compared to the inequalities of class status.

Helen Mayer Hacker

Hacker considers women a minority group and provides an alternative approach. She explains the 'minority group' as:

> any group of people who because of their physical and cultural characteristics, are singled out from others in the society in which they live for differential and unequal treatment, and who therefore regard themselves as objects of collective discrimination.

By comparing the situation of American Blacks and women, Hacker indicates some of the advantages of classifying the latter as a minority group. First, both groups have high social visibility. Second, both groups have similar ascribed attributes which are assigned to them by the majority group simply on the grounds of their minority group membership. Third, the status of both, Blacks and women, is rationalized in similar ways by the majority group. Fourth, both groups adopt accommodating behaviour in adopting their situation. Finally, both groups suffer from similar discriminatory practices.

According to Hacker, all these features reflect in the existing position of women in the broader society.

Marx and Engels

Both Marx and Engels believed that they were witnessing the beginnings of women's liberation in nineteenth century capitalist society. They argued that the demand for female wage labour would raise the status and power of proletarian women within the family. Marx believed that despite its many evils, capitalist industry creates a new economic foundation for a higher form of the family and of relations between the sexes. Female employment would largely free women from economic dependence upon their husbands and so from male dominance within the family.

Engels took a similar view maintaining that with female wage labour, the last remnants of male domination in the proletarian home have lost a foundation—except, perhaps, for some of the brutality towards women which became firmly rooted with the establishment of monogamy. However, the bourgeois wife in capitalist society was still required to produce heirs and so forced to submit to male control.

Marx and Engels believed that true equality between the sexes could only be achieved in a socialist society in which the forces of production were communally owned. In this context, the bourgeois wife would not be mere property for the production of heirs, since there would be no privately owned wealth for them to inherit. The onerous duties of housework and motherhood would no longer be performed by individual women since all work was the responsibility of the community. In Engels' words "Private housekeeping is transformed into social industry."

Women's Liberation

From the late 1960s, a vast literature was produced in support of the women's liberation in totality. Many of the famous feminist writers were socialist in orientation. However, they go beyond a simple socialist solution, maintaining that the abolition of private property will not automatically result in women's liberation. They proposed a kind of 'socialist feminism' which involved not only an attack on the economic class structure, but also a direct attack on all forms of male domination.`

3

METHODOLOGY

Nature of Study

The present survey was carried out to know the reality of the phenomenon of gender discrimination prevailing in the rural society of Kashmir. This has been done because it is evident from all primary and authentic sources available that women in Kashmir in general, and in rural areas in particular, faced acute and various problems including negative discrimination at all levels and in many fields. However, in the recent past, multifarious processes of modernization and development have led to fundamental and significant degree of change in the rural areas of Kashmir. Consequently, like other major groups in society, women in these areas have experienced certain positive degree of change. Moreover, this situation has put serious challenges to the traditional pattern of life of women, particularly the pattern of discrimination related to them. In this wider social context, this survey intended to focus on various aspects of gender discrimination in two important districts of Budgam and Baramulla in the state of Jammu and Kashmir.

Universe of Survey

The situation of gender discrimination prevails more or less in all parts of the Kashmir valley. However, the intensity of this phenomenon reveals more in the rural areas in comparison to the urban areas. This difference in degree can be explained in terms of broader and deeper impact of education, mass media, socio-economic mobility, other cultures and so on. It is essentially in this context that two districts of Budgam and

Baramulla were selected for survey. On the one hand, this will reveal the traditional pattern of gender discrimination and, on the other hand, will portray exert reality, of change in this pattern. While the Baramulla district stands forward relatively in education, economic, social, developmental and other relevant fields, the district Budgam's standing is different, if not on the other extreme. Again, while the former district is highly rural and occupies border area, the latter district is significantly urban and (some parts of it) forms part of the capital city of Srinagar. This have given a representative character to the areas selected for this survey.

Selection of Respondents

The theme and objectives of the survey became the basis for selection of respondents in both districts. While respondents were selected by random sampling, the sample represented all social categories such as age, sex, economic, social, educational and other relevant groups. Thus, the sample of respondents was highly representative. In total, 688 respondents were selected for the survey whose composition reveals in Tables 3.1 and 3.2.

Methods/Techniques of Investigation

In order to carry out a realistic survey on the concerned topic, the respondents were approached through questionnaire and interview. A detailed and comprehensive questionnaire was prepared by the UNICEF experts (with very minor changes) and that was given to the literate respondents. The necessary help for filling the questionnaire was provided by research investigators. At the same time, illiterate respondents were interviewed in the local Kashmiri language and their respective response was entered in the questionnaire by research investigators. The set of questionnaires, meant for different categories of respondents, composed questions of open-ended and fixed-choice types, depending upon the nature of questions. The questionnaire broadly consisted of five following sections:

(i) Personal and Family Information;

(ii) Education and Work;

TABLE 3.1

DISTRIBUTION OF SAMPLE IN BARAMULLA DISTRICT

Sl.No.	Name of Block	Q. Naire No. 1 (Among Women)	Q. Naire No. 2 (Among men)	Q. Naire No. 3 (Among girls)	Q. Naire No. 4 (Village Leader)	Q. Naire No. 5 (P.S. Teacher)	Q. Naire No. 6 (Ang. W.W.)	Q. Naire No. 7 (A.N. M)	Total
1.	Baramulla	12	08	04	01	01	01	01	23
2.	Pattan	12	08	04	01	01	Nil	01	27
3.	Tangmarg	12	08	04	01	Nil	01	01	27
4.	Wagoora	12	08	04	01	01	01	Nil	27
5.	Booniyar	12	08	04	01	01	01	Nil	27
6.	Rafiabad	12	08	04	01	Nil	01	01	27
7.	Sopore	12	08	04	01	01	01	Nil	27
8.	Zainageer	11	08	04	Nil	01	01	01	26
9.	Bandipara	11	08	04	01	01	01	01	27
10.	Hajan	11	07	04	Nil	01	01	01	25
11.	Sumbal	11	07	04	01	01	01	01	26
12.	Rihma	11	07	03	01	01	01	01	25
13.	Uri	11	07	03	01	01	01	01	25
14.	Gurej	-	-	-	-	-	-	-	-
	Total	150	100	50	11	11	11	11	344

TABLE 3.2

DISTRIBUTION OF SAMPLE IN BUDGAM DISTRICT

Sl.No.	Name of Block	Q. Naire No. 1 (Among Women)	Q. Naire No. 2 (Among men)	Q. Naire No. 3 (Among girls)	Q. Naire No. 4 (Village Leader)	Q. Naire No. 5 (P.S. Teacher)	Q. Naire No. 6 (Ang. W.W.)	Q. Naire No. 7 (A.N. M)	Total
1.	Budgam	20	13	7	2	2	2	2	48
2.	B.K. Pora	20	13	7	2	2	2	2	48
3.	Nagam	19	13	6	2	2	2	2	46
4.	Khan Sahab	18	12	6	1	1	1	1	40
5.	Beeru	19	13	6	1	1	1	1	42
6.	Khag	18	12	6	1	1	1	1	40
7.	Narbal	18	12	6	1	1	1	1	40
8.	Chadoora	18	12	6	1	1	1	1	40
	Total	150	100	50	11	11	11	11	344

(iii) Man-Woman Work;

(iv) Health; and

(v) Other Issues.

Efforts were made on the part of research investigators to record the most correct version of the response put forward by a variety of respondents.

Field-Investigation

The survey was carried out successfully through extensive fieldwork in two districts of Baramulla and Budgam. All tehsils and blocks in these districts were covered in the fieldwork. Even the blocks/tehsils where weather (and other) conditions were not conducive for carrying out research were covered. Only the Gurez block could not be covered because the areas was cut off from the rest of the world due to heavy snowfall. In the first stage, research investigators made general field visits and contacted notables and other important/influential persons in these areas. This helped in developing much needed rapport with the respondents. In the second stage, 15 research investigators (from Department of Sociology, University of Kashmir, Srinagar) held detailed investigations in two districts during the period of 3-4 months.

Data Processing and Analysis

The information/data collected during field investigation was aggregated and tabulated according to set themes and objectives of the survey. In order to explain/analyse relevant information/data, the questions were given codes which were decoded later on. Similarly, the needs of the survey. Finally, the explanation/analysis of collected information/data paved the way for finalization of the report of survey.

Organization of the Seminar in Srinagar

The final draft of the survey was submitted to the UNICEF, New Delhi in December 1996, through the concerned agency of J&K Government. After going through contents of this survey, the UNICEF suggested to organize a national seminar in Srinagar with the following broader objectives:

(i) to present and discuss all major findings of the survey before the local, regional and national audience of concerned academicians, experts, bureaucrats, planners, women activists, governmental and non-governmental organizations, social welfare administrators, representatives of rural development agencies/organizations and so on;

(ii) to invite critique of these findings in the light of experience and expertise of the experts belonging to various fields of life;

(iii) (in the context of presentation and discussion of findings of the survey) to prepare specific set of recommendations for the state and central governments and various UN agencies to negate and debase the phenomenon of gender discrimination.

Accordingly, a three-day national seminar was organized on the topic Gender Discrimination in the Kashmir Valley at Sher-i-Kashmir International Convention Complex, Srinagar on 2-4 August, 1997.

Limitations and Difficulties of the Survey

It may be highly relevant at this stage to mention about several prolems faced by research investigators and the director at the stages of investigation and explanation/interpretation. Firstly, the most serious problem faced by all was predetermined nature of the questionnaire. It refers to the problem whose origin lies in the questionnaire. While several questions were irrelevant and wrong in the Kashmir context, many questions of primary importance were missing, therefore inherent limitations in the questionnaire remained there and thereby distorting the response of some potential respondents. Secondly, the then prevailing militancy conditions put some serious limitations on the survey. Accordingly, while some questions could not be posed to the respondents, other questions attracted misleading response. For example, the questions on abortion and family planning got highly misleading response. Third, there is a basic problem faced by the researchers which is related to the availability of primary source, authentic and correct data about the women's situation in Kashmir. In fact, very less and not authentic information/data is available in this regard. It is partly because no census was carried out in 1991, in J&K state and partly because no academic studies was carried out in this field. The available data from the government sources is incorrect and highly unreliable. But, in the present situation, when information/data from any other source is not available, one has no alternative except to depend on government sources.

4

BUDGAM AND BARAMULLA DISTRICTS A Profile

Total Population 1991

The districts of Budgam and Baramulla compose significant number of total population in Jammu and Kashmir state. This reflects in the estimates of total population, density of population, and proportion of these districts' population to the total population in the state in the year 1991. All these estimates are mentioned in Table 4.1.

TABLE 4.1

ESTIMATED POPULATION IN J&K STATE 1991 (BY DISTRICT)

Sl. No.	*Districts*	*Estimated** Population*	*Density per sq. km.*	*Percentage of the State's Total Population*
1.	Anantnag	826291	207	10.70
2.	Pulwama	516441	369	6.69
3.	Srinagar	892506	401	11.56
4.	Budgam	497346	363	6.44
5.	Baramulla	861214	188	11.15
6.	Kupwara	416404	175	5.39
7.	Leh	89474	2*	1.15
8.	Kargil	81067	6	1.05
9.	Jammu	1207996	390	15.65
10.	Udhampur	602807	132	7.80
11.	Doda	525326	45	6.80
12.	Kathua	492288	186	6.37
13.	Rajouri	417333	159	5.40

Sl. No.	*Districts*	*Estimated*** *Population*	*Density per sq. km.*	*Percentage of the State's Total Population*
14.	Poonch	292207	175	3.78
15.	State	7718700	76*	100

Source: *Digest of Statistics,* 1991-92 (published by Directorate of Economics and Statistics, J&K Government).

Total Population 1981

In order to have a comparative view of population dynamics in Budgam and Baramulla districts and J&K state at large over a period of two decades, it seems highly relevant to see various population figures of 1981 the following table shows necessary details in this regard:

Table 4.2 reveals that, in terms of total population in the J&K state in 1981, while Budgam district stands at number 8, Baramulla district stands at number 3. While the former district composed 6.44 per cent and the latter composed 11.15 per cent of the total population in the state in that year. These two districts jointly composed 17.59 per cent of the total population.

While Budgam district had 85.87 per cent and 14.13 per cent of rural and urban population respectively, the same proportion in Baramulla district was 86.60 and 13.40 respectively. It follows that the Budgam district had more urban population and other urban features in comparison with the Baramulla district. Consequently, the density of population in the former district was higher than it prevailed in the latter district.

Pattern of Population Growth

The figures in above tables reveal clearly that population increase in these two districts and the state at large, has been phenomenal. This aspect of population reflects in Table 4.3.

TABLE 4.2

AREA. DENSITY, RURAL/URBAN, MALE/FEMALE POPULATION IN J&K STATE (DISTRICTWISE) 1981

Districts	Area (sq. km)	Population									Density (Per sq. km.)
		Rural			Urban			Total			
		Persons	Male	Female	Persons	Male	Female	Persons	Male	Female	
Anantnag	3984	586065	310563	275502	70286	37143	33143	656351	347706	308645	165
Pulwama	1398	367799	194025	173774	36279	19068	17211	404078	213093	190985	289
Srinagar	2228	138133	73343	64790	570195	304846	265349	708328	378189	330139	318
Budgam	1371	315377	167656	147721	51885	27739	24146	367262	195395	171867	268
Baramulla	4588	580376	310282	270094	89766	48011	41755	670142	358293	311849	146
Kupwara	2379	319055	171646	147409	9688	5263	4455	328743	176909	151834	138
Leh	*82665	59662	31216	28446	8718	5032	3686	68380	36248	32132	2**
Kargil	14036	62465	33603	28862	3527	2006	1521	65992	35609	30383	5
Jammu	3097	663751	343747	320004	279644	148225	131419	943395	491972	451423	305
Udhampur	4550	410389	215041	195348	43247	22922	20325	453636	237963	215673	100
Doda	11691	400088	209704	190384	25174	13658	11516	425262	223362	201900	36
Kathua	2651	327133	170406	156727	41990	22164	19826	369123	192570	176553	134
Rajouri	2630	286667	149988	136679	15833	8691	7142	302500	158679	143821	115
Poonch	1674	210026	111193	98833	14171	7479	6692	224197	118672	105525	134
State	**222236	4726986	2492413	2234573	1260403	672247	588156	5987389	3164660	2822729	59

Source: Census Department. J & K Government. 1992-93.

TABLE 4.3

PATTERN OF POPULATION GROWTH, 1951-1991

Unit	*1951*	*1961*	*1971*	*1981*	*1991 Estimated*
J & K	3253852	3560976	4616632	5987389	7718700
Baramulla	359526	392192	517900	670142	861214
Budgam	189881	213918	269033	167262	497346

Source : Digest of Statistics, 1991-92 (published by Directorate of Economics and Statistics, J&K Government).

Sex and Rural/Urban Composition

Table 4.4 shows the sex and rural/urban composition of the population in Budgam and Baramulla districts and the State in the year 1981.

Table 4.4 reveals that while Budgam district had 85.87 per cent and 14.13 per cent rural and urban population respectively in the year 1981, the Baramulla district composed 86.60 per cent and 14.40 per cent of the same. These figures reflect the similarity in major population trends (especially related to the areas mentioned in the table) in the concerned districts. Agains, more or less, similar situation emerges in the sex composition.

Literate Population

Table 4.5 presents a comprehensive picture about literacy prevailing in Budgam and Baramulla districts and J&K state in the year 1981.

Table 4.5 reveals clearly that there exist very low literacy rates in comparison with the state and national literacy rates. The table also reveals that literacy rates stand higher among males than among the females. It is also denotes that literacy rates in these districts stand higher in urban than rural areas. Another revealing aspect of the above table is that literacy rate in all areas, among all groups/communities/classes and age/ sex groups has increased in the recent past.

Religious Composition of Population

The religious composition of population in Budgam and Baramulla districts and J&K state in 1981 has been mentioned in the Table 4.6

TABLE 4.4

COMPOSITION OF MALE/FEMALE AND RURAL/URBAN POPULATION, 1981

Unit	*Total Population*	*Rural*				*Urban*			
		Male		*Female*		*Male*		*Female*	
		No.	*Percentage*	*No.*	*Percentage*	*No.*	*Percentage*	*No.*	*Percentage*
J&K	5987388	2492413	41.62	2234573	37.32	672247	11.22	588156	9.82
Baramulla	670142	310282	46.30	270094	40.30	48011	7.16	41755	6.23
Budgam	367262	167656	45.65	147721	40.22	27739	7.55	24146	6.57

Source : Digest of Statistics (published by Directorate of Economics and Statistics, J & K Government).

TABLE 4.5

LITERATE/ILLITERATE POPULATION, 1981

Unit	Total	Rural				Urban				Total				Literate Population as percentage of Total Population
		Male		Female		Male		Female		Male		Female		
		No.	%age	No.	%age	No.	%age	No.	%age	No.	%age	No.	%age	
J&K	5987389	788581	3.17	233902	3.90	359988	6.01	210305	3.57	1148569	19.18	448207	7.48	26.67
Baramulla	670142	84241	12.57	17396	2.59	24114	3.59	12450	1.85	108335	16.16	29846	4.45	20.62
Budgam	367262	38649	10.52	7485	2.03	13151	3.58	6299	1.71	51800	14.10	13784	3.75	17.86

Source : Digest of Statistics, 1991-92 (Published by Directorate of Economics and Statistics, J & K Government).

TABLE 4.6

RELIGIOUS COMPOSITION OF POPULATION, 1981

Unit	*Hindus*	*Sikhs*	*Muslims*	*Christians*	*Budhists*	*Jains*	*Other Religious Group*	*Total*
	No.	*No.*	*No.*	*No.*	*No.*	*No.*	*No.*	*No.*
J&K	1930448	133675	3843451	8481	69706	1576	44	5987389
	(32.24%)	(2.23%)	(64.19%)	(0.14%)	(1.16%)	(0.02%)	(.00073%)	-
Baramulla	13513	9806	6,46,707	106	2	8	-	670142
	(2.01%)	(1.46%)	(96.50%)	(0.015%)	(0.0002%)	(0.001%)	-	
Budgam	9642	5158	352355	96	11	-	-	367262
	(2.62%)	(1.40%)	(95.94%)	(0.026%)	(0.0029%)	-	-	

Source : Digest of Statistics, 1991-92 (Directorate of Economics and Statistics, J &K Government).

Table 4.6 reflects the existing religious plurality in all areas of the state including the Budgam and Baramulla districts. Thus, it is evident that Muslims, Sikhs, Hindus, Christians and others live in both these districts and contribute to the composite character of the valley. However, the Muslims constitute a dominant position in the valley and the state in comparison to other minority religious communities.

Villages and Towns

There has been a general observation that the process of urbanization has started, though slow in degree, in Budgam and Baramulla districts in the recent decades. In addition to other consequences, this process has contributed towards the transformation of villages into towns. The nature of this change is evident in the Table 4.7

TABLE 4.7

NUMBER OF VILLAGES AND TOWNS, 1971 AND 1981

	Villages						*Towns*	
	1971			*1981*			*1971*	*1981*
Unit	*I*	*U.I*	*Total*	*I*	*U.I*	*Total*		
J&K	6503	239	6742	6477	281	6758	45	58
Baramulla	659	16	675	646	14	660	5	6
Budgam	484	20	504	475	21	496	-	1

Source : Digest of Statistics 1991-92 (Directorate of Economics and Statistics, J&K Government).

I - Inhabitant

UI - Unhabitant

The figures in Table 4.7 confirms that while the number of villages have decreased, the number of towns have increased, though slowly. In Budgam district, there were 504 villages and no town in 1971, but the number of villages has come down to 496 and the number of towns rose to 01 in 1981. Similarly, in Baramulla district in 1971, there were 675 villages and 5 towns. Later on, in 1981, while the number of villages came down to 660, the number of towns increased to 6. It follows that a significant degree of urbanization has occurred in both these districts in the previous decade/s.

Working Force Population

Table 4.8 conveys the number of working population in Budgam and Baramulla districts and J&K state in the year 1981:

The 4.8 reflects clearly that the dominant proportion of population in Budgam and Baramulla districts belonged to the categories of primary, secondary and territory workers. It is primarily because these two districts are rural in nature/ character. The table also reveals that there are significant number of main and marginal workers living in these two districts. Moreover, majority of the working force composed mainly of the males in comparison with the females.

Occupation of the Workers

Table 4.9 gives the information about the occupation of inhabitants (sex-wise) in Budgam and Baramulla districts and J&K state in the year 1981:

Table 4.9 clearly reveals that the dominant majority of people living in these two districts are involved directly or indirectly in agriculture-related activities. In agriculture-dominated economy, they are engaged as workers in different statuses and in different areas. There are other areas, which are numerically insignificant, in the people in these rural areas work as petty-workers and on petty wages.

Development of Education

Number of Educational Institutions

Since the education in J&K state from primary to university stage is free, the state government was compelled to provide all necessary facilities (both monitary and non-monitary facilities) for the growth and development in this regard in the post-1947, decades. Consequently, these state-sponsored efforts had led to certain degree of progress in the state. An important aspect of educational development, i.e., the increasing number of educational institutions, in Budgam and Baramulla districts is shown in detail in Tables 4.10 and 4.11.

Table 4.10 and 4.11 reveal higher as well as increasing number of educational institutions at all educational levels and in ail educational fields in the year 1996. While Budgam district had total number of 744 educational institutions 529 for boys

TABLE 4.8

NUMBER OF WORKING FORCE BY SEX, 1981

	Main Workers			*Marginal Workers*			*Non Workers*			*Workers as percentage to Total Population*
Unit	*Male*	*Female*	*Total*	*Male*	*Female*	*Total*	*Male*	*Female*	*Total*	
J&K	1651846	166725	1818571	114369	717104	831473	1398445	1938900	3337345	30.37
Baramulla	192501	18119	210620	10500	83424	93924	155292	210306	365598	31.43
Budgam	110551	9944	120495	4042	54441	58483	80802	107482	188284	32.81

Source : Digest of Statistics 1981 (Published by Directorate of Economics and Statistics, J&K Government).

TABLE 4.9

OCCUPATION OF POPULATION (SEXWISE), 1981

Occupation	*J&K*		*Budgam*		*Baramulla*	
	Male	*Female*	*Male*	*Female*	*Male*	*Female*
Cultivators	928027	105870	63231	3924	110518	10727
Agricultural Labourers	59890	3650	3157	49	8013	118
Fishing and Hunting Live Stock Forestry	59438	4861	2426	47	6644	227
Mining and Kurrying	3209	87	117	-	461	-
Manufacture Servising and Household Industry	78600	17732	13193	3710	13314	4092
Processing and Repairs	99957	8092	8427	1357	10359	1227
Constructions	49827	1886	2437	6	5601	8
Trade and Commerce	99829	1576	3585	47	9986	206
Transport Storage and Communications	56677	759	2632	13	4739	14
Other Services	216393	22415	11215	761	22865	1199
Total	1651846	166729	110554	9944	192501	18119

Source: Department of Economics and Statistics, J&K Government.

TABLE 4.10

NUMBER OF EDUCATIONAL INSTITUTIONS IN BUDGAM DISTRICT, 1996

Sl.No.	*Zone*	*Higher Secondary School*		*High School*		*Middle School*		*Central School*		*Primary School*		*Mobile Primary School*		*Total*	
		B	*G*	*B*	*G*	*B*	*G*	*B*	*G*	*B*	*G*	*B*	*G*	*B*	*G*
1.	Budgam	01	01	04	04	08	04	02	01	31	17	--	--	46	27
2.	Khansaheb	01	--	03	--	09	03	02	--	35	06	02	--	52	09
3.	Draygam	--	--	05	01	06	01	01	--	29	10	--	--	41	12
4.	Soi-Bugh	--	--	07	01	06	02	02	--	37	21	--	--	52	24
5.	Chadoora	01	--	04	--	14	04	--	02	23	16	02	--	44	22
6.	Nagam	01	--	05	01	09	03	02	--	15	15	01	--	31	19
7.	Chrar-i-Shrief	01	--	02	01	09	01	01	--	25	04	01	--	39	06
8.	B.K. Pora	03	01	03	02	16	09	01	--	26	21	--	--	49	33
9.	Beerwah	01	01	04	--	08	03	02	--	32	11	--	--	47	15
10.	Hardapanzoo	--	--	03	--	08	--	01	--	35	07	02	--	49	07
11.	Magam	02	--	03	01	11	05	--	--	32	12	--	--	48	18
12.	Narbab	--	--	03	01	10	02	--	01	18	19	--	--	31	23
	Grand Total	11	03	44	12	114	37	14	04	338	159	08	--	529	215

Source: Chief Education Office, Budgam, Jammu and Kashmir Government.

TABLE 4.11

NUMBER OF EDUCATIONAL INSTITUTIONS IN BARAMULLA DISTRICT, 1996

Sl.No.	*Zone*	*Higher Secondary School*		*High School*		*Middle School*		*Central School*		*Primary School*		*Mobile Primary School*		*Total*	
		B	*G*	*B*	*G*	*B*	*G*	*B*	*G*	*B*	*G*	*B*	*G*	*B*	*G*
1.	Jullan	--	--	4	--	5	1	2	--	25	11	4	--	40	12
2.	Uri	1	1	3	--	3	3	3	--	33	10	1	--	43	14
3.	Chandan Wari	--	--	5	--	5	3	3	--	26	14	3	--	42	17
4.	Boniyar	1	--	3	--	5	2	1	--	29	11	2	--	41	13
5.	Fateh Garh	--	--	3	--	5	1	2	--	31	6	--	--	41	7
6.	Baramulla	1	1	6	1	10	12	--	1	15	18	--	--	32	33
7.	Singh Pora (K)	--	--	4	2	3	4	1	--	20	6	3	--	31	12
8.	Wagoora	1	--	4	2	9	3	1	1	33	6	1	-	49	12
9.	Nehalpora	--	--	4	--	7	3	--	--	39	9	--	--	50	12
10.	Pattan	1	--	3	1	6	1	1	2	25	13	--	--	36	17
11.	Singh Pora Pattan	--	--	5	--	4	3	3	1	21	18	--	--	33	27
12.	Kunzer	--	--	3	1	9	2	2	--	33	12	--	--	47	15
13.	Tangmarg	1	--	2	1	7	3	1	--	33	12	3	--	47	16
14.	Hajin	1	--	3	2	6	3	1	--	26	16	--	--	37	21
15.	Sumbal	2	-	3	1	8	4	1	-	29	11	-	-	43	16
16.	Sopore	1	1	8	2	4	5	4	3	24	17	--	--	41	28

Sl.No.	*Zone*	*Higher Secondary School*		*High School*		*Middle School*		*Central School*		*Primary School*		*Mobile Primary School*		*Total*	
		B	*G*	*B*	*G*	*B*	*G*	*B*	*G*	*B*	*G*	*B*	*G*	*B*	*G*
17.	Danger Pora	1	--	5	1	11	6	2	--	27	19	--	--	46	26
18.	Rohama	1	--	3	1	13	5	1	2	25	9	--	--	43	17
19.	Bandi Pora	--	1	4	--	4	6	4	--	51	15	--	--	63	22
20.	Quilmuqam	1	--	5	1	6	3	--	--	38	27	--	--	50	31
21.	Dangiwacha	1	--	3	1	9	3	1	--	25	15	--	--	39	19
22.	Gurez	1	--	5	1	3	--	2	--	37	6	--	--	48	7
	Total	15	4	88	18	142	75	36	10	645	281	17	0	943	388

Source: Chief Education Office, Baramulla, Government of Jammu & Kashmir.

and 215 for girls) in 1996, Baramulla district had 1331 educational institutions (943 for boys and 388 for girls) in the same year. In addition to these institutions, there were 3 degree colleges in Baramulla district, on Jawahar Navodividwlla school in Budgam and one in Baramulla districts. During the investigation, most of the concerned government officials quoted an estimate according to which there exists one primary school in every 3 kilometre radius in these districts. Moreover, there were hundreds of educational institutions functioning in these districts run by private agencies/organizations/individuals. The number of estimate about these institutions are not available.

Enrolment of Students in Schools

With the heavy increase in the number of educational institutions, the number of children (both, boys and girls) too increased heavily. This reflects in Table 4.12 regarding enrolment of students in various schools in Budgam and Baramulla districts in the year 1994-95:

TABLE 4.12

ENROLMENT OF STUDENTS IN EDUCATIONAL INSTITUTIONS AT VARIOUS LEVELS, 1994-95

Class	*Budgam*			*Baramulla*		
	Boys	*Girls*	*Total*	*Boys*	*Girls*	*Total*
1.	7711	4306	12017	11110	7783	18893
2.	7299	4461	11760	8663	6251	14914
3.	6715	4122	10837	8164	5463	13627
4.	4876	2602	7478	7398	4991	12389
5.	3342	2010	5352	6334	4374	10708
6.	3921	1760	5681	5471	2824	8295
7.	3698	1727	5425	5287	2818	8105
8.	3313	1583	4896	4908	2638	7546
9.	3101	1412	4513	4983	3309	8292
10.	2927	1273	4200	4420	2215	6635
11.	1360	557	1917	3051	1304	4355
12.	2168	727	2895	1875	807	2682
Total	50431	26540	76971	71664	44777	116441

Source : Chief Education Offices, Budgam and Baramulla Districts, J & K Government.

Table 4.12 reveals heavy enrolment of students in all educational institutions at all levels and in all fields in both districts. This is absolutely in contrast with the situation which prevailed before 1947. In the Budgam district, the total enrolment in the schools was 76,971 (50,431 boys and 26,540 girls) in 1994-95, while in Baramulla district, the students enrolment in school was 116,441 (71,664 boys and 44,777 girls) in the same academic year.

Enrolment in Technical Institutes

According to Table 4.12, there was tremendous increase in the enrolment of students in all fields, including the technical fields. The details in this regard are given in Tables 4.13, 4.14 and 4.15.

TABLE 4.13

ENROLMENT OF STUDENTS IN TECHNICAL INSTITUTES (SUBJECTWISE) IN BARAMULLA DISTRICT, 1995-97

Sl.No.	*Subjects*	*Boys*	*Girls*	*Total*
1.	Electrician	20	-	20
2.	Radio and T.V.	18	-	18
3.	Plumber	08	-	08
4.	Computer	14	2	16
5.	Welder	03	-	03
6.	Painting	-	-	-
7.	Motor Mechanic	17	-	17
8.	Carpentary	06	-	06
9.	Fitter	-	-	-
10.	Turner	-	-	-
11.	Cutting and Tailoring	-	41	41
12.	Stenography	19	17	36
13.	Tractor Mechanic	23	-	23
	Total	128	60	188

Source : District Administration, Baramulla District, J & K Government.

TABLE 4.14

ENROLMENT OF STUDENTS IN TECHNICAL INSTITUTES (SUBJECTWISE) IN BUDGAM DISTRICT, 1995-96

(A) Industrial Training Institute for Women (Budgam)

Sl.No.	*Subjects*	*Boys*	*Girls*	*Total*
1.	Radio and TV	-	19	19
2.	Electronics	-	41	41
3.	Stenography	-	28	28
4.	Computer	-	34	34
5.	M/C Knitting	-	16	16
	Total	00	138	138

(B) Industrial Training Institute (Budgam)

Sl.No.	*Subjects*	*Boys*	*Girls*	*Total*
1.	Cutting and Tailoring	-	12	12
2.	Stenography	12	05	17
3.	Electrician (Ist year)	23	-	23
	(IInd year)	13	-	13
4.	Radio and TV	19	-	19
5.	Electronics	33	02	35
6.	Motor Mechanic	30	-	30
7.	Turner	03	-	03
8.	Welder	05	-	05
	Total	174	19	193

Source : District Administration, Budgam District, J & K Government.

TABLE 4.15

ENROLMENT OF STUDENTS IN WOMEN'S POLYTECHNIC IN BUDGAM DISTRICT, 1993-1996

Sl.No.	*Subjects*	*Ist year*	*IInd year*	*IIIrd year*	*Total*
1.	Electronics and Communication Engineering	20	-	21	41
2.	Costume Designing and Garment Technology	13	2	13	28
3.	Computer Engineering	15	-	-	15
4.	Secretarial Practice and Office Management	21	-	-	21
5.	Nursery and Primary Teachers Training	08	-	-	08
	Total	77	2	34	113

Source : District Administration, District Budgam, J & K Government.

Number of Teachers

Continuing the above-mentioned trends in the field of education, the teachers (both male and female) have emerged as a significant group in Budgam as well as in Baramulla districts. The details in this regard are shown in Table 4.16.

TABLE 4.16

NUMBER OF TEACHERS, 1996

	District Budgam			*District Baramulla*		
Level	*Male*	*Female*	*Total*	*Male*	*Female*	*Total*
Primary	787	500	1287	950	565	1515
Middle	966	330	1296	1155	569	1724
High	634	161	795	1268	291	1559
Hr. Sec.	206	74	280	412	61	473
Total	2593	1065	3658	3785	1486	5271

Source : Chief Education Office, Budgam and Baramulla districts, J&K Government.

Budgetry Allocation for Education

The above-mentioned increasing trends in the field of education has been possible due to the allocation of funds to the educational growth in the annual budgets and five year plans consistently. The relevant details have been given in Table 4.17.

Health Conditions

Availability of Health Centres

All governments in the J&K state, irrespective of political and ideological differences, followed the broader objective related to the development of health culture among people belonging to all areas, regions, groups and communities. These broader objectives were followed by establishing the system of health centres at the village, block, tehsil and district levels and making available all necessary medical facilities. Special care was taken to provide all necessary facilities to women, especially at the time of delivery. Table 4.18 shows the number of health centres and health facilities available therein in Budgam and Baramulla districts in the year 1996:

Table 4.18, based solely on official information, reveals significant growth of health centres and medical facilities therein

TABLE 4.17

BUDGETRY ALLOCATION FOR EDUCATION, 1990-1994

	District Budgam					District Baramulla				
Level	*1994-95*	*1993-94*	*1992-93*	*19991-92*	*1990-91*	*1994-95*	*1993-94*	*1992-93*	*1991-92*	*1990-91*
Primary	396.69	330.23	275.13	244.56	213.23	476.96	174.00	157.29	206.06	198.04
Middle	453.90	378.25	315.10	273.64	238.63					
High	480.90	400.75	334.10	290.44	253.74	195.23	208.20	164.98	153.31	144.05
Hr. Sec.	252.20	210.15	116.71	147.57	128.40					

Source : District Administration Budgam and Baramulla Districts J&K, Government.

TABLE 4.18

NUMBER OF HEALTH CENTRES AND FACILITIES AVAILABLE IN BUDGAM AND BARAMULLA DISTRICTS, 1996

Sl.No.		*PHC's*		*CHC's*		*S.D. Hosp.*		*District Hospital*	
		Baramulla	*Budgam*	*Baramulla*	*Budgam*	*Baramulla*	*Budgam*	*Baramulla*	*Budgam*
1.	Number	27	26	1	4	4	-	1	1
2.	Total beds	150	150	30	80	120	-	110	20
3.	Total beds for women in Gyn/Obs	13	35	6	20	12	-	20	6
4.	Total wards	1 (each)	30	2	8	16	-	7	4
5.	Total No. of beds for women Gyn/Obs.		4	1	4	4	-	1	1
6.	Total no. of beds for women in wards		20		40		-		10
7.	Total MO's in position	29	36	7	8	30		18	88
8.	Total women MO's in position	5	11	2	5	6	-	3	23
9.	Total number of men occupying beds in 93-94	2397	150	301	320	3002	-	4226	237
10.	Total No. of women occupying beds in 93-94	2796	161	356	301	3597	-	1795	241
11.	Total posts of nurses sanctioned	22	22	6	28	17	-	17	07
12.	Nurses in position	17	-	4	-	15	-	14	06
13.	Total mid-wives post sanctioned	9	26	1	4	4	-	1	02
14.	Mid-wives in position	6	-	1	4	4	-	1	02
15.	Deliveries conducted	287	169	349	272	623	-	680	320
16.	Still births	23	2	17	2	28	-	22	03
17.	Abortions	3	0	23	1	31	-	26	03

Source: Chief Medical Offices, Budgam and Baramulla districts, J&K Government.

TABLE 4.19

NUMBER OF MEDICAL STAFF, 1998

Sl. No.	*ANM Posts*	*Baramulla*	*Budgam*	*Baramulla*	*Budgam*	*Baramulla*	*Budgam*
		Sanctioned		*In position*		*Vacant*	
1.		261	196	221	156	40	40
2.	MPW Male	10	11	8	11	2	nil
3.	Sub Centres	Own Accomodation		Rented			
		7	7	152	118		

Source: Chief Medical Offices, Budgam and Baramulla districts J & K Government.

for men and women. The Table 4.19 gives the statistical information about the number of medical and para-medical staff (especially related to women's problems) in Budgam and Baramulla districts in 1996:

Health Centres/Facilities Available

Table 4.20 conveys the exact number of health centres and the nature of health facilities available in the two districts in 1996:

TABLE 4.20

AVAILABILITY OF HEALTH CENTRES AND FACILITIES, 1996

Sl.No.	*Institutions/facilities available*	*Budgam*	*Baramulla*
1.	District hospitals	01	01
2.	Sub-district hospitals	04	04
3.	Community health centres	04	01
4.	Primary health centres	26	27
5.	Sub-centres	125	177
6.	Allopathic dispensaries	14	29
7.	Unani dispensaries	26	48
8.	Private/voluntary institutions	-	04
9.	Total women medical officers	16	12
10.	Total beds in district hospitals	20	110
	(a) Beds for women Gyn./Ob.	05	20
	(b) Beds for women others	05	30
11.	Total beds in sub-district hospitals	80	120
	(a) Beds for women Gyn./Ob.	20	12
	(b) Beds for women/others	20	-
12.	Total No. of Gynaecologists	02	01
	(a) POHs sanctioned	05	08
	(b) Total Gynaecologist currently in position	02	01
13.	Total MO posts in PHC/CHC	44	36

Source: Chief Medical Offices, Budgam and Baramulla districts J&K Government.

Development Activities

Beneficiaries of Various Schemes

Various schemes were initiated by the central and state governments to improve the conditions of life of people, especially the women, living in rural and urban areas. Many such schemes were introduced and implemented in Baramulla and Budgam districts in the previous decades. Consequently, many people, particularly women, in these districts got benefited. The information in this regard is portrayed in Tables 4.21 to 4.24.

TABLE 4.21

TRYSEM BENEFICIARIES, BARAMULLA DISTRICT (LAST FIVE YEARS)

Scheme	*1990-91*		*91-92*		*92-93*		*93-94*		*94-95*	
	M	*F*	*M*	*F*	*M*	*F*	*M*	*F*	*M*	*F*
Type shorthand	-	07	20	08	03	05	90	-	52	-
Sozni	-	-	-	-	-	20	-	160	-	240
Crewel	-	-	-	-	-	20	-	190	-	290
Knitting	-	-	-	-	-	-	-	142	-	222
Total	-	07	20	08	03	45	90	492	52	752

Source : District Administration Baramulla District, J&K Government.

TABLE 4.22

PMRY BENEFICIARIES, BUDGAM DISTRICT (1994-1995)

Sl. No.		*Male*	*Female*	*Total*
1.	Number of candidates selected	31	25	336
2.	Number of sponsored to the banks	229	15	244
3.	Number of cases sanctioned	24	1	25

Source: Department of Industries, District Budgam, J&K Government.

Handicraft Centres

Table 4.25 shows the variety/nature and number of handicraft centres established and run by the governmental agencies/organizations in Budgam and Baramulla districts during the period 1988-1995:

Unemployment of Males and Females

Table 4.26 shows the number of unemployed persons, both males as well as females, who had registered in the district employment office in Budgam upto 1995:

Social Welfare Schemes

Destitute Women's Homes

Women's welfare stands as one of the important areas in social welfare schemes. In order to provide maximum benefits

TABLE 4.23

DWCRA BENEFICIARIES, BUDGAM DISTRICT (1991-1994)

Block	*B.K Pora*	*Beerwah*	*Khag*	*Budgam*	*Narbal*	*Chadoora*	*Khan Sahab*	*Nagam*
Year of Introduction	1994	1994	1991	1992	1994	1994	1994	1994
Total groups formed	03	06	09	12	06	06	03	05
Total members	41	75	159	168	80	107	44	70
Number of groups registered	03	06	08	10	6	06	03	05
Total membership of registered groups	41	75	144	148	80	107	44	70
Total groups for which Ist dose of revolving fund released	03	06	09	12	06	06	03	05
Total groups who have received 2nd dose of revolving fund	-	01	01	04	-	-	-	-
Total groups inactive	-	06	07	06	-	01	03	-
Total groups active	03	-	01	04	06	05	-	05
Total groups who have approached banks for credit	-	-	-	-	-	-	-	-
Total groups who have got bank credit	-	-	-	-	-	-	-	-

Source : District Administration, District Budgam, J&K Government.

TABLE 4.24

DWCRA BENEFICIARIES, DISTRICT BARAMULLA (1994-1996)

Block	*Pattan*	*Rohama*	*Baramulla*	*Soporo*	*Boniyar*	*Bandipora*	*Rafiabad*	*Zaingeer*	*Uri*	*Hajin*	*Wagoora*	*Tang marg*	*Sumbal*
Year of Introduction	*95-96*	*95-96*	*94-95*	*94-95*	*94-95*	*94-95*	*94-95*	*94-95*	*94-95*	*94-95*	*94-95*	*94-95*	*94-95*
Total groups formed	01	03	26	19	06	05	04	01	01	06	04	01	01
Total members	14	30	296	122	66	54	44	10	11	80	48	10	10
Number of groups registered	-	-	-	-	-	-	-		-	-	-	-	-
Total membership of registered groups	-	-	-	-	-	-	-	-	-	-	-	-	-
Total groups for which Ist dose of revolving fund released	01	03	26	19	06	05	04	01	01	06	04	01	01
Total groups who have received 2nd dose of revolving fund	-	-	15	12	05	05	03	01	01	06	03	-	-
Total groups active	01	03	all	19	06	05	04	01	01	06	04	01	01
Total groups inactive	-	-	-	-	-	-	-	-	-	-	-	-	-
Total groups who have approached banks for credit	-	-	-	-	-	-	-	-	-	03	-	-	-
Total groups who have got bank credit	-	-	-	-	-	-	-	-	-	-	-	-	-

Source: District Administration, District Baramulla, J&K Government.

TABLE 4.25

NUMBER OF PERSONS TRAINED IN HANDICRAFT CENTRES/TRADES (1988-1995)

Subject	*Budgam*						*Baramulla*					
	88-89	*89-90*	*90-91*	*91-92*	*93-94*	*94-95*	*88-89*	*89-90*	*90-91*	*91-92*	*93-94*	*94-95*
Carpet	25	20	25	21	44	25	1250	1250	1250	1250	1250	1250
Gabba	-	-	-	-	-	-	75	75	75	75	75	75
Wood carving	250	200	250	205	198	250	25	25	25	25	25	25
Corni shawl	50	36	50	35	22	25	25	25	25	25	25	25
Suzni shawl	275	252	275	250	280	300	200	200	200	200	200	200
Cribble (Crewel)	350	302	350	319	330	350	150	150	150	150	150	150
Chain stitch	150	138	150	141	168	175	125	125	125	125	125	125
Tapestry	175	152	175	161	165	175	100	100	100	100	100	100
Calico printing	-	-	-	-	-	-	25	25	25	25	25	25
Paper mache	200	190	200	188	175	200	50	50	50	50	50	50
Art stapple	-	-	-	-	-	-	125	125	125	125	125	125

Source: Department of Handicrafts, District Baramulla, J&K Government.

TABLE 4.26

NUMBER OF UNEMPLOYED PERSONS REGISTERED IN DISTRICT EMPLOYMENT OFFICE, BUDGAM UPTO 1995

Level of Education	*1990*		*1991*		*1992*		*1993*		*1994*		*1995*	
	Male	*Female*	*Male*	*Female*	*Male*	*Female*	*Male*	*Female*	*Male*	*Female*	*Male*	*Female*
Middle Pass	714	82	617	73	782	35	742	72	372	32	819	44
Matric/PUC	2019	427	2114	596	1630	490	1460	570	2107	672	1263	827
Hr. Sec./TDC	1210	721	1029	621	1493	450	1435	493	1915	577	1532	415
BA/BSc	522	302	472	319	685	329	689	335	699	372	798	412
MA/MSc	114	108	117	82	153	228	135	101	122	107	311	122

Source: District Employment Office, District Budgam, J&K Government.

TABLE 4.27

FUNCTIONING OF DESTITUTE WOMEN'S HOMES, 1994-1995

Sl. No.	*Particulars*	*Budgam*			*Baramulla*	
1.	Name of the institution	*MFI Khansahib	**NN Chadoora	MFI Handipara	MFI Uri	MFI Baramulla
2.	Set up in which year	1986	1988	N.A.	N.A	N.A
3.	Total seats/Capacity	25 inmates	25 inmates	55	55	25
4.	Total number of resident widows	-	-	20	26	15
5.	Total number of orphans	4 inmates	4 inmates	05	07	04
6.	Total number of those neither widows nor orphans but otherwise eligible	21 inmates	21 inmates	15	19	11
7.	Total expenditure in the year 1994-95	2.766 lakhs	3.005 lakhs	6931 in both homes	2.1 lakhs	
8.	Total non-salary/wage expenditure in the year 1994-95	1595lakhs	152 lakhs	4515 in both homes	1.12 lakh	

Source : Department of Social Welfare, District Budgam, J&K Government.

to the under-priviledged and disadvantaged women, several schemes and programmes were introduced. The establishment of destitute women's homes stands as one of the prominent schemes in this regard. Table 4.27 gives information about the functioning of these homes in Budgam and Baramulla districts in the year 1994-1995:

Old-Age Pension Scheme

This scheme was introduced to provide various benefits to the old-age people, especially women, in Budgam and Baramulla districts. Table 4.28 gives details about the benefits provided by this scheme to the women:

TABLE 4.28

BENEFITS PROVIDED BY OAPS, 1995-1996

Sl.No.	*Scheme*	*Budgam*	*Baramulla*
1.	Total beneficiaries so far under old age/widows/scheme	Not available	7100
2.	Number of women	2105 as on 24.4.96	4732

Source : Department of Social Welfare Districts, Budgam and Baramulla, J&K Government.

Vocational Training Centres and Courses

In order to make women able to earn and become economically independent, the government established several vocational training centres in the villages and towns in Budgam and Baramulla districts. Tables 4.29 and 4.30 give details about the establishment of vocational centres and training courses they impart:

TABLE 4.30

VOCATIONAL TRAINING CENTRES AND TRAINING COURSES PROVIDED IN BUDGAM DISTRICT

		Total trained in the year				
Sl.No.	*Subject*	*1994-95*	*93-94*	*92-93*	*91-92*	*90-91*
1.	Social Welfare centres	225	250	250	250	250
2.	Cottage industry centre (Carpentry trade)	25	25	25	25	25
3.	Cottage industry centre (Willow works)	25	-	25	25	25

Source: Department of Social Welfare, District Budgam, J&K Government.

TABLE 4.29

VOCATIONAL TRAINING CENTRES AND TRAINING COURSES PROVIDED IN BARAMULLA DISTRICT

Subject	*Year*	*Total No. of Trainees in Each Centre*	*Vocational Centre*	*Total Trained During the Year*
Cutting and tailoring centre	1991-92	25	14	340
C.I.C (Carpentry)		25	01	25
Cutting and tailoring centre	1992-93	25	14	350
C.I.C. (Carpentry)		25	01	25
Cutting and tailoring centre	1993-94	25	14	340
C.I.C. (Carpentry)		25	01	25
Cutting and tailoring centre	1994-95	25	14	350
C.I.C. (Carpentry)		25	01	25
Cutting and tailoring centre	1995-96	25	14	350
C.I.C. (Carpentry)		25	01	25

Source : Department of Social Welfare, District Baramulla, J&K Government.

OBC/SC-ST Scholarships

In order to help girls to pursue formal education till the matric stage and in different fields, a scheme of scholarships was introduced in Budgam and Baramulla districts. The girls belonging to OBC and SC/ST categories were of special focus of this scheme. In this regard, Tables 4.31 and 4.32 reveal the relevant information in Budgam and Baramulla districts.

TABLE 4.31

OBC/SC-ST SCHOLARSHIP BENEFICIARIES, BUDGAM DISTRICT

Sl.No.	*Subject*	*90-91*	*92-93*	*93-94*	*94-95*	*95-96*
1.	Total No. of scholarships given in last five years	9	1820st	1865st	1919st	3000st
2.	Number of girls among beneficiaries	9	599st	880st	615st	1019st

Source : Social Welfare Office, Budgam District, J & K Government.

TABLE 4.32

OBC/SC-ST SCHOLARSHIP BENEFICIARIES, BARAMULLA DISTRICT

Scheme	*92-93*	*Girls*	*93-94*	*Girls*	*94-95*	*Girls*	*95-96*	*Girls*
Pre-matric	1695	568	2233	764	2592	798	2404	918
Physically Handicapped	185	50	244	62	145	40	176	68
Re-impursment of fee	28	11	33	14	33	20	48	14
Mochi-Watal scholorship	101	25	86	34	93	35	84	28
Special Stipend	93	34	147	27	84	25	87	23
Industrial training Institute	41	21	35	15	23	11	26	11
Stipend to the students whose father are engaged in unclean occupation	-	-	-	-	112	45	133	48

Source : Social Welfare Office, Baramulla District, J&K Government.

5

FINDINGS : WORK AND EDUCATION IN KASHMIRI SOCIETY

The Kashmiri society, especially in the rural context, is generally a tradition-dominated and tradition-upholding society. As is the case with many traditional societies in Asia, there prevails widespread and deep-rooted discrimination against the female sex in the Kashmiri society. This situation certainly leads to basic disadvantages and hurts the process of their progress and development. However, the fact of equal importance stands that the traditional pattern of sex discrimination has undergone significant degree of change in the previous five decades due to various factors. This transformation has enabled women to change the traditional lifestyle and play a different role and maintain a different status in the family and the broader society.

In the above context, the attainment of modern education has necessarily emerged as one of the significant factors for this type of change in women in rural as well as urban Kashmir. In other words, modern education has provided possibilities for basic and potential change among women. In actuality, the attainment of modern education by girls has necessarily led to the adoption of new role and status within and outside their homes. In this background, a close and positive relationship has emerged between modern education and adoption of work by women. It follows that if the women attain modern education, they develop new role/s and adopt new jobs, especially outside their homes. On the other hand, if they remain uneducated, they continue with traditional role and status within and outside their homes.

In the traditional Kashmiri society, women in general did not get education. They performed traditional roles/jobs within and outside their homes. In the rural areas, in addition to their domestic/household jobs, women helped actively in the economic activities in the family. In the rural areas, in addition to their domestic/household jobs, women helped their men at the agricultural fields. However, changing situation in the previous decades, especially attainment of modern education by women even in backward/underdeveloped areas and lower socio-economic groups and classes, led to the emergence of new roles/jobs for educated women. Moreover, other factors, especially ongoing modernization and development processes intensified and accelerated the change among major groups of women in rural and urban areas. The cumulative effect of this situation was that women at large underwent certain irreversible processes of change in their traditional role and status. Though, this change has occured lesser in degree, it stands crucial because it has initiated broader processes of change among women on sound basis. Within this totality of changing environment, the traditional pattern of discrimination against the female sex underwent certain degree of change which reflects in the response of respondents entered in Table 5.1.

TABLE 5.1

PREFERENCE FOR GIRLS' EDUCATION (BARAMULLA AND BUDGAM)

Sl. No.	*Class Upto Which Girls Should Read*	*Baramulla*		*Budgam*		*Total*	
		Men	*Women*	*Men*	*Women*	*Number*	*Percentage*
1.	Upto V	00	30	00	00	30	6
2.	VI to VIII	18	25	20	17	80	16
3.	IX to X	12	15	15	13	55	11
4.	XII	15	25	23	26	89	17.8
5.	Upto Graduation	00	25	32	54	111	22.2
6.	More	55	25	10	40	130	26
7.	Others	00	00	00	00	00	0
8.	No Education	00	05	00	00	05	1
	Total	100	150	100	150	500	100

Table 5.1 reveals that 495 out of 500 (99.00 per cent) respondents showed clear preference for girls, education in both districts, whereas only 5 out of 500 (01.00 per cent) respondents gave opposite response. The former response can be explained in terms of widespread impact of ongoing processes of change and development in the villages, the latter response can be explained to cultural, religious and other related factors. However, it must be noted here that complete opposition to the girls' education has died down completely. Even most-conservative and extreme-religious individuals have compromised with the ongoing full education to girls.

Table 5.1 also reveals that significant number of respondents, i.e., 130 out of 500 (26.00 per cent), preferred graduation and higher education (i.e., masters, doctoral research and professional/technical/specialized education) for their girls and other females, whereas 111 out of 500 (22.00 per cent) respondents preferred their family females' education upto graduation only. These responses can be related to the respondents' level of education, degree of exposure, cultural transformation and socio-economic mobility. Again while 89 out of 500 (17.8 per cent) respondents preferred girls' education upto 12th standard, 80 out of 500 (16.00 per cent) respondents consented their females' education upto 8th standard only. This response can also be explained in terms of above factors. However, one important fact which revealed from these responses at large was that both sexes equally favoured attainment of modern education by women. In actuality, completely favourable social ethos has been developed in all villages in this regard. Though there is near total support for women's education at all levels and in all fields, the existing reality reveals that more boys than girls get education (and have been educated) in these districts (see relevant tables in the previous chapter). This fact reveals the underlying reality according to which girls face negative discrimination (probably unconsciously) at the hands of their parents/guardians and other male elders in their families.

More or less same situation (explained in the preceding section) prevails in these districts *vis-a-vis* the preference for boys' education. While every respondent favours equal education to boys and girls, more boys than girls get formal education in the educational institutions. Moreover, girls at lower levels maintain equal or near-to-equal proportion in the schools, but this (proportion) decreases when they move upwards, i.e., towards higher classes. In this connection, our investigation brought forth information which reveals in Table 5.2.

TABLE 5.2

PREFERENCE FOR BOYS' EDUCATION (BARAMULLA AND BUDGAM)

Sl.No	*Class Upto Which Girls Should Read*	*Baramulla*		*Budgam*		*Total*	
		Men	*Women*	*Men*	*Women*	*Number*	*Percentage*
1.	Upto V	00	15	00	00	15	3
2.	VI to VIII	00	10	00	00	10	2
3.	IX to X	02	10	00	00	12	2.4
4.	Upto XII	16	09	21	37	83	16.6
5.	Upto Graduation	19	31	17	41	108	21.6
6.	More	63	70	62	72	267	53.4
7.	Others	00	00	00	00	00	0
8.	No Education	00	05	00	00	05	1
	Total	100	150	100	150	500	100

Table 5.2 reveals that 495 out of 500 (99.00 per cent) respondents favoured boys' education, even on priority basis, while 5 out of 500 (1.00 per cent) respondents gave opposite response. The latter respondents did not oppose boys education, but they emphasized specifically on equal favour to girls education. The totality of this response was explained by the respondents in terms of material needs which boys fulfill after getting education. In many cases, it revealed that boys felt compelled to get education upto medium level only in order to make themselves available for earning which is needed badly by the family. A significant number of respondents, 267 out of 500 (53.40 per cent) preferred boys' education upto above-graduation level, which includes professional, technical and other standard courses. The reasons cited for this response were given as "boys need this level of education" and "they have to work for earning money for themselves and their

families". Even the women respondents' response in this regard was not much different. A less significant number of respondents (108 out of 500; 21.60 per cent) wanted boys' education upto the graduate level. These respondents belonged mostly to the middle and lower classes and they need the income of their children after they complete graduation.

Nearly all respondents favoured boys' education upto graduation even outside their villages/towns and the state of J&K. But, in the case of girls, such type of education was not favoured by all. The reasons for this type of response have been mentioned in the preceding section. In addition, our investigation revealed that 83 out of 500 (16.60 per cent) respondents wanted boys' education upto 12th standard only. It was partly because parents wanted them to help in enhancing their income and partly because parents need them in agricultural and non-agricultural activities. As revealed in the previous section, in this response, there seemed not much difference in the responses of males and females. The district-wise and tehsil-wise responses too were more or less similar. In this way, it reveals clearly that though, women suffer in some areas and at certain levels, there seems very little organized efforts to discriminate women.

In the changing situation in these two districts, there prevailed absolutely no opposition to the attainment of modern education on the part of boys and girls. In fact, a favourable social environment in this regard has developed in this regard. After a specific investigation, it revealed that there was no opposition for attainment of modern education by girls. When a question about resistance to the attainment of modern education by girls was asked, the dominant number of respondents, (450 out of 500; 90.00 per cent), in both districts said that "they have no reason to resist the attainment of modern education on the part of boys as well as girls." At the same time, 50 out of 500 (10.00 per cent) respondents gave no response. This silence on the part of some respondents is meaningful. We infer that they oppose the attainment of modern education by girls, but can not make it public in view of strong pro-education environment.

At large, the above responses show that there prevails an overwhelming support for modern education by both sexes. This positive response can be related to the cumulative effect of the processes of modernization, especially modern education, mass media, political participation, economic growth-development, cultural exposure, demographic transformation, social mobility and so on. It is important to note here that, in this situation, even religion and culture are used to help boys and girls in their educational attainment. The respondents repeated the factor of religion again and again saying that it inspires as well as instructs the attainment of education.

However, it is important to note that opposition to the attainment of modern education, especially by girls at the higher stage, has not died down completely. The ongoing process of modern education to boys and girls alike and together is criticized mainly on cultural and religious grounds. The religious argument presented by some respondent was that "since women have to stay at home and as dependent, they need not go for education." This opposition is also levelled against equal status given to boys and girls in modern education. The respondents said that "since women are not equal to men, they must not be provided status and role equal to men." The rationale of the above also reveals in the following arguments presented by respondents:

(a) boys have to play primary and dominant role in the family and outside;

(b) girls' education is not necessary because they are dependent throughout their lives;

(c) boys have to do business and earn for the family necessarily at the earlier stage comparatively;

(d) boys have natural superiority over girls;

(e) restrictions need to be imposed forcefully on girls;

(f) boys have to face competition in qualification and merit than girls;

(g) boys need to fulfill needs of all family members.

It is important to note here that differences in responses have social, economic, cultural, religious, educational, psychological and other bases. While majority of men support equal education to boys and girls at all stages, majority of women support differential and segregated education to boys and girls. While the men respondents belonged to all classes and groups, the women respondents were from educated, exposed and economically well-off groups. Again, elder age-group and religious-oriented groups opposed equal and mixed-education to boys and girls, less religious and younger age-groups supported that type of education. These inter-generational differences reflected in other responses too.

As has happened in other societies, the attainment of modern education had crucial and irreversible impact on the practices related to marriage in rural Kashmir. A set pattern of impact of modern education on the traditional practices of marriage such as endogamy and exogamy can be cited in this regard. In the rural Kashmir context, the impact of education has been experienced in terms of positive or negative implications. Our investigation in district Budgam and Baramulla revealed the relevant response entered in the Table 5.3.

TABLE 5.3

IMPACT OF EDUCATION ON MARRIAGE PRACTICES (BUDGAM AND BARAMULLA)

Sl.No.		*Baramulla*		*Budgam*		*Total*	
		Men	*Women*	*Men*	*Women*	*Number*	*Percentage*
1.	Helpful	79	100	58	81	318	63.6
2.	Hindrance	00	10	00	00	10	2
3.	Does not matter	08	25	10	20	63	12.6
4.	Cannot say	13	15	32	49	109	21.8
	Total	100	150	100	150	500	100

Table 5.3 reveals that dominant majority of respondents (i.e., 318 out of 500; 63.30 per cent) felt that attainment of modern education proved helpful in their marriages, while 10 out of 500 (2.00 per cent) respondents felt otherwise. The former type of response may be explained in terms of getting better/qualified/rich/urban-based husbands/wives. This pattern of impact had serious and basic implications for the existing pattern of gender

discrimination in Kashmir. The latter type of response is practically ignorable and came from economically lower classes and socially backward (occupational) communities. Table 5.3 also reveals that 109 out of 500 (21.80 per cent) respondents showed no response, but 63 out of 500 (12.60 per cent) respondents said that education does not matter much in their context. In fact, there are many occupational and agricultural communities in Kashmir in which attainment of modern education, especially at the higher level, is not needed much for the performance or improvement in their status. However, as mentioned earlier, 63.60 per cent respondents were of the opinion that attainment of modern education proved or can prove helpful in their own or relatives' marriages. In actuality, modern education in itself has emerged as a desirable value in the marriage market in Kashmir. The reasons they cited in support of their response included good match, lesser amount of dowry, increase in the possibility of mutual adjustment, heavy increase in the family income, emergence of elevated role-status of women, encouragement of children's good education, more respect for the couple, good family-household management, extremely helpful to women at all stages of their lives, especially during pregnancy and at the time of child bearing and child rearing.

The third and fourth responses in Table 5.3 came specially from socially-economically lower classes/groups and illiterate sections. In reality, they do not go for attainment of modern education, but join their traditional and hereditary occupations at very early stage of life. So, the impact of education among these groups is minimal and ignorable.

Responses in Table 5.3 clearly reveal that a significant proportion of respondents and their children do not go for modern education. This situation prevails despite the fact that education from primary till university level is free in the state. In this context, a relevant and pointed question regarding reason/reasons for not getting modern education on the part of respondents' children was asked. The reasons cited by the respondents included the following:

(i) poverty situation;

(ii) no encouragement from the parents;

(iii) higher drop-out rate at the primary-middle levels;

(iv) engaging children in handicraft centres;

(v) earning for the family at the younger age;

(vi) no consciousness about the benefits of getting education;

(vii) favourable environment not provided by the governmental agencies and organizations;

(viii) low social estimation; and

(ix) lack of educational facilities.

These reasons/factors have to be assessed/evaluated in the context of the situation wherein education is free and almost every second or third village in the state has one primary school. The state government claims that at least one primary school in an area of one kilometre has been established in the state. The above-mentioned reasons can be categorized as:

(a) economic reasons (cited by 87.00 per cent respondents),

(b) cultural/social reasons (cited by 9.00 per cent respondents), and

(c) other reasons (cited by 4.00 per cent respondents).

It follows that the economic reason is the most significant reason for not sending children, especially girls, to schools at an early age. Other reasons have secondary importance.

The gender discrimination generally reveals in the works performed by males and females in the society. In addition to being an existing reality, this phenomenon prevails at the ideational level too. In this background, people develop categories of work for men and for women which are different and exclusive. This categorization of works for girls and boys exclusively affects the work-pattern in the broader society, which also reveals the nature of gender discrimination. In this regard, we enquired about the attitudes of respondents of this survey towards different/exclusive works performed by men and women. The response we received has been shown in the Tables 5.4 and 5.5.

TABLE 5.4

DIFFERENT TYPES OF WORK DONE BY BOYS AND GIRLS (BARAMULLA DISTRICT)

Sl.No.	*Name of the Work*	*Only Girls*		*Only Boys*		*Both*		*Neither*	
		Men	*Women*	*Men*	*Women*	*Men*	*Women*	*Men*	*Women*
1.	Looking after siblings	55	87	18	00	00	38	08	25
2.	Fetching water	80	76	00	00	32	03	08	42
3.	Cooking	55	78	00	00	55	20	52	--
4.	Washing clothes	75	124	00	00	05	13	20	13
5.	Washing vessels	71	88	00	20	09	00	20	42
6.	Shopping	00	03	51	48	16	87	33	12
7.	Looking after animals	09	05	61	67	43	50	07	34
8.	Grazing animals	00	00	78	141	10	04	12	05
9.	Collecting fire wood	43	66	00	19	47	00	10	65

TABLE 5.5

DIFFERENT TYPES OF WORK DONE BY BOYS AND GIRLS (BUDGAM DISTRICT)

Sl.No.	*Name of the Work*	*Only Girls*		*Only Boys*		*Both*		*Neither*	
		Men	*Women*	*Men*	*Women*	*Men*	*Women*	*Men*	*Women*
1.	Looking after Siblings	33	80	00	00	67	47	00	23
2.	Fetching water	69	93	00	00	31	00	00	57
3.	Cooking	100	145	00	00	00	01	00	04
4.	Washing clothes	38	98	01	00	61	51	00	10
5.	Washing vessels	25	148	00	00	75	02	00	00
6.	Shopping	00	00	11	41	87	109	02	00
7.	Looking after animals	03	41	05	73	92	36	00	00
8.	Grazing animals	00	103	87	35	10	12	03	00
9.	Collecting fire wood	87	41	00	41	13	59	00	09

The above tables reveal that people have pre-determined and set attitudes towards different kinds of jobs performed by different sexes. For example, the job of looking after siblings was viewed by the respondents as the job of girls (only) whose number was 274 out of the total sample of 500 (54.80 per cent). On the other hand, the same job was viewed as the job of boys (only) by 18 out of 500 (13.60 per cent) respondents. In comparison to these two attitudinal responses, 152 out of 500 (30.20 per cent) respondents considered this job as the job of boys as well of girls. In totality, these responses reveal that dominant majority of respondents (i.e. 54.00 per cent) felt that this job was exclusively meant for girls/women. This dominant response is supported by the prevailing cultural, religious, social and other relevant attitudes. Despite some considerable changes in the villages, this pattern of attitudes still prevail and necessarily affects the nature of gender discrimination. Similarly, 378 out of 500 (75.60 per cent) respondents were of the opinion that the job of cooking should be done by girls exclusively. However, there were 76 out of 500 (15.20 per cent) respondents who opined that cooking work should be done by both sexes. This response can be further explained by the fact that this work has always remained the exclusive job of the female folk. So, they are traditionally considered as good managers of kitchen. With regard to shopping, majority of the respondents (299 out of 500; 59.80 per cent) wanted that both sexes must do this work, while 151 out of 500 (30.20 per cent) respondents favoured this work for boys only. About 9.00 per cent (47/500) respondents wanted to retain this work for elders of both sexes in comparison to their youngsters.

In general, the responses in Tables 5.4 and 5.5 reveal:

- set pattern of attitudes *vis-a-vis* different kinds of works, which are based on socio-economic factors;
- family and household-related works are favoured for female sex;
- out-family and labour-needed works are meant for the male sex;

- socio-economic bias and class differences of the respondents and
- changes in the recent decades have been adopted partly.

The existing gender bias in the broader society also reveals in the prevailing types/patterns of marriage which prove advantageous/disadvantageous to women. This may specifically be observed in the factor age of marriage for boys/girls. In this regard, we asked a specific question. The response we received reflects in the Table 5.6.

TABLE 5.6

AGE OF MARRIAGE FOR BOYS AND GIRLS (BUDGAM AND BARAMULLA)

		Girls		*Boys*	
	Marriagable Age Group	*Budgam*	*Baramulla*	*Budgam*	*Baramulla*
Response of Men	18-20 years	47	29	12	16
	20-22 years	23	23	08	11
	23-25 years	12	15	21	30
	25-27 years	10	23	47	38
	28-30 years	08	10	12	05
Response of Women	18-20 years	37	21	22	26
	20-22 years	21	43	27	35
	23-25 years	49	54	18	47
	25-27 years	31	26	39	41
	28-30 years	12	06	44	01

Table 5.6 reveals that men respondents in general found the following marriagable age for men:

(a) 25-27 years by 85/500 (42.50 per cent) respondents;

(b) 23-25 years by 51/500 (25.10 per cent) respondents;

(c) 18-20 years by 28 (14.00 per cent) respondents;

(d) 20-22 years by 19 (9.50 per cent) respondents; and

(e) 28-30 years by 17 (8.50 per cent) respondents.

At the same time, the appropriate age group quoted for girls by men is as follows:

(a) 18-20 years by 76 (38.00 per cent) respondents;

(b) 20-22 years by 46 (23.00 per cent) respondents;

(c) 25-27 years by 33 (16.00 per cent) respondents;

(d) 23-25 years by 27 (13.00 per cent) respondents; and

(e) 28-30 years by 18 (9.00 per cent) respondents.

The Table 5.6 and above explanation reflect the following points of sociological relevance:

(i) While the most-preferred groups in marriage-market are 25-47 and 23-25 years age groups, the least preferred groups belong to 20-22 years age groups, the least preferred groups belong to 20-22 and 28-30 years age groups;

(ii) The traditional patterns of marriage continue and change in this field has proved partial

(iii) The responses cannot be explained in terms of class only. Other factors have contributed equally or more to the emergence of the situation.

On the other hand, the women respondents felt that the marriagable age of men are as follows:

(a) 25-27 years by 80 (26.60 per cent) respondents;

(b) 23-25 years by 65 (25.60 per cent) respondents;

(c) 20-22 years by 62 (20.60 per cent) respondents;

(d) 18-20 years by 48 (16.00 per cent) respondents;

(e) 28-30 years by 45 (15.00 per cent) respondents.

Similarly, the age groups quoted for marriage for girls by women respondents are as follows:

(a) 23-25 years by 103 (34.30 per cent) respondents;

(b) 20-22 years by 64 (21.30 per cent) respondents;

(c) 18-20 years by 58 (19.30 per cent) respondents;

(d) 25-27 years by 57 (19.00 per cent) respondents; and

(e) 28-30 years by 18 (6.00 per cent) respondents.

6

FINDINGS : WORK PERFORMED BY MEN AND WOMEN IN KASHMIRI SOCIETY

The women/girls in the Kashmiri society, like in other developing countries in Asia, perform certain particular types/forms of work within and outside their homes. It has been observed that there prevails certain set attitudes/notions regarding the performance of works by women. In this background, while some works are characterized as 'feminine works,' other works are seen as 'masculine works.' These attitudes are rooted in the broader society and are determined by social, economic, cultural, religious and other factors. In addition to other aspects, these attitudes reflect certain set pattern of attitudes and works related to the phenomenon of gender discrimination in the broader society. In the Kashmir context, all such propositions apply. In actuality, the prevailing pattern of the performance of works by men and women reflect the existing pattern of works by men and women reflect the existing pattern of gender discrimination here. In this regard, when we enquired from our respondents, they showed the response noted in Table 6.1.

Table 6.1 reveals that a maximum number of respondents, i.e., 314 out of 500 (62.80 per cent), are of the opinion that the family farming is done by women either to earn money or to help their families. In actuality, the most common work performed by women in rural areas was the family farming. It has been observed that they usually work in the fields side by side with their male family members. Our investigation also reveals that 197/500 (35.80 per cent) respondents felt that the female-folk work at the dairy farms for the reasons referred in the preceding

TABLE 6.1

WORKS PERFORMED BY MEN AND WOMEN (BARAMULLA AND BUDGAM)

Sl. No.	Name of Work	Baramulla		Budgam		Total
		Men	Women	Men	Women	
1.	Family Farming	56	125	98	35	314
2.	Dairy	40	60	17	80	197
3.	Sheep Rearing	16	15	47	25	103
4.	Work in Orchards	45	55	51	37	188
5.	Wage labour in agriculture	04	40	00	08	52
6.	Wage labour in Orchards	07	15	03	18	43
7.	Wage labour in Carpet Weaving	25	30	17	35	107
8.	Wage labour in Shawl embroidery	20	95	21	55	191
9.	Producing handicraft items	12	35	12	15	74
10.	Trade	00	00	00	00	00
11.	Other wage labour	00	00	00	00	00
12.	Service/Salary	30	41	41	21	133
13.	Others	00	00	00	00	00

response. Similarly, 52/500 (10.20 per cent) respondents believe that number of rural women are engaged as wage labourers in agricultural activities. It has also been noted that 188/500 (37.60 per cent) respondents were working in the orchards, where they do easier and less-manual jobs. In addition, the rural women are actively participating in areas such as sheep-rearing, carpet-weaving, shawl-embroidery and governement/private services. However, the contribution of women to trade and commerce in rural areas is nil. As per the views of our respondents, this response may be explained in terms of inhibitions of some works for women and the notion that women must not perform hard and manual works.

The data in Table 6.1 reveals sufficiently that women in rural areas and in traditional situations seem highly productive in economic, social and other fields. In reality, they have significantly and continuously contributed to the economic and social status of their families. But, this role/status is generally neither acknowledged nor reciprocated in rural areas.

The overall response in the table is that women in rural Kashmir are active in all fields, especially economic. It is also important to note that they work side by side with their male family members, especially in the fields. But, at the same time, the fact of equal importance is that this crucial role of women is neither acknowleded nor reciprocated. It is also not paid as it deserves. It is primarily because the works in rural areas are not valued as they deserve. So, there seems consciousness, and the resultant action, on the part of rural men in this regard.

In the rural areas in the Kashmir valley, the dominant majority of women are involved in agricultural and fruit-growing activities, in addition to their household activities. This is the situation in Budgam and Baramulla districts too. In our investigation among the rural respondents about the activities performed by males and females in the agricultural and fruit-growing fields, we found that both the sexes are actively involved in different jobs related to these sectors and sub-sectors. The details of these activities performed by men and women in our areas of investigation are noted in Tables 6.2 and 6.3.

TABLE 6.2

ACTIVITIES PERFORMED BY MALES/FEMALES IN AGRICULTURAL AND FRUIT-GROWING FIELDS (DISTRICT BARAMULLA)

Sl.No.	*Name of Activities*	*Mainly Done by Women*		*Mainly Done by Men*		*Both Response of*	
		Men	*Women*	*Men*	*Women*	*Men*	*Women*
1.	Field of preparation	00	00	65	85	35	65
2.	Sowing	00	00	75	95	25	30
3.	Weeding	00	05	45	60	55	85
4.	Transplanting	00	10	16	20	84	120
5.	Applying fertilizers	00	13	49	95	51	42
6.	Applying pesticides	00	00	63	103	37	47
7.	Harvesting/plucking	16	40	30	15	54	95
8.	Processing (Dry etc.)	16	40	30	15	54	95
9.	Winnowing	12	25	40	55	48	70
10.	Threshing	00	00	27	69	73	81
11.	Packing	00	11	70	103	80	36
12.	Sale to traders	00	00	70	148	30	02
13.	Seed management	13	27	55	00	32	14

TABLE 6.3

ACTIVITIES PERFORMED BY MALES/FEMALES IN AGRICULTURAL AND FRUIT GROWING FIELDS (DISTRICT BUDGAM)

Sl.No.	Name of Activities	Mainly Done by Women		Mainly Done by Men		Both Response of	
		Men	*Women*	*Men*	*Women*	*Men*	*Women*
1.	Field preparation	00	00	87	49	13	101
2.	Sowing	00	00	87	131	13	19
3.	Weeding	08	00	12	137	80	13
4.	Transplanting	11	10	05	17	84	123
5.	Applying fertilizers	00	00	47	129	53	21
6.	Applying pesticides	00	00	43	111	57	39
7.	Harvesting/plucking	00	00	23	09	77	141
8.	Processing (Dry etc)	06	81	31	00	63	69
9.	Winnowing	13	13	27	51	60	86
10.	Threshing	00	00	12	102	88	48
11.	Packing	00	00	100	110	00	40
12.	Sale to traders	00	00	100	143	00	07
13.	Seed management	00	10	100	43	00	97

Table 6.3 reveals clearly that women in the villages perform certain major activities within and outside their families. According to our investigation, while women in Baramulla district work mainly in the areas such as transplanting, harvesting, processing, weeding and threshing (see Table 6.2 in Budgam district they work in the areas which include field preparation, transplanting, harvesting, packing and processing (see Table 6.3). In general, the response in both districts show that women there participate in agricultural activities significantly. But, at the same time, it is correct that while men usually work in some specific areas, women too prefer to work in other specific areas. In other words, they rate their specific area of activity. In other words, they rate their specific area of activity. Our enquiry in two districts in this regard revealed the rating of works/activities by men and women as follows:

CLASSIFICATION OF WORKS RELATED TO AGRICULTURE AND FRUIT GROWING FIELDS

Women's Works	*Men's Works*
Processing (drying)	Sowing
Winnowing	Selling to traders
Seed Management	Field preparation
Transplantation	Applying fertilizers
Weeding and applying	Packing
Fertilizers	

Tables 6.2 and 6.3 response of respondents in both districts show that heavy majority (of respondents) are in favour of sharing various works in agriculture. In addition to other aspects, this response also indicates that women are capable of working/sharing with their male counterparts satisfactorily. This response came from both the sexes belonging to various groups and classes.

Men and women in the rural areas in Kashmir also work in the area of animal husbandry. In actuality, the work in this area stands as the significant occupation of the village women after agriculture. The work in this area is done not only for economic gains, but also for the family consumption. The distribution of work between men and women in this specific area is revealed in Tables 6.4 and 6.5.

Tables 6.4 and 6.5 reflect that a dominant majority of respondents (/500 per cent) favour women to be the core actors in the area of animal husbandry. In general, the respondents like women to work at home, in non-labour intensive fields and in areas in which family's basic and immediate needs are fulfilled. Moreover, the above tables reveal clearly that major areas of activity for women are cleaning sheds, giving feed, providing water to animals, milking, sheering, processing milk products and selling milk. On the other hand, it seems that not many men are interested in performing such activities. Thus, a lesser percentage of them are engaged in activities such as giving water, milking, shearing, caring for sich animals and processing milk products. In the light of these responses, we are in a position to establish the rating of the activities performed by men and women related to animal husbandry. The rating follows:

CLASSIFICATION OF ACTIVITIES RELATED TO ANIMAL HUSBANDRY

Activities Performed by Men	*Activities Performed by Women*
Grazing	Milking
Buying feed	Giving water and shearing
Decision to buy/sell animals	Giving feeds Cleaning sheds
Processing wool	Preparing feed
Preparing feed Cleaning sheds	Decision to buy/sell animals
Giving feed	Caring for sick animals

The above rating pattern of activities related to animal husbandry and performed by men and women reflect some points which follow. First, women in rural areas participate in equal or more proportion in various activities related to animal husbandry. Second, women perform same kind of activities as their menfolk in many cases. Third, while most of the out-home activities are performed by men, the in-home activities are performed by both, men and women alike. Fourth, most of the labour intensive, but less time-consuming activities are

TABLES 6.4

ACTIVITIES PERFORMED BY MEN AND WOMEN IN ANIMAL HUSBANDRY (DISTRICT BARAMULLA)

Sl.No.	*Name of Activities*	*Mainly Done by Women*		*Mainly Done by Men*		*Both Response of*	
		Men	*Women*	*Men*	*Women*	*Men*	*Women*
1.	Cleaning sheds	15	44	24	04	04	15
2.	Preparing feed	04	52	27	04	09	04
3.	Buying feed	01	12	36	11	03	37
4.	Giving feed	26	49	08	02	06	09
5.	Giving water	25	51	10	04	05	05
6.	Milking	31	47	06	03	03	10
7.	Shearing	22	40	08	13	10	07
8.	Grazing	01	08	36	48	03	04
9.	Caring for sick animals	10	20	08	07	31	33
10.	Deciding to buy/sell animals	06	11	21	38	13	11
11.	Processing milk products	34	53	03	05	03	02
12.	Processing wool	00	-	05	06	00	-
13.	Selling milk	08	14	30	41	02	15

TABLE 6.5

ACTIVITIES PERFORMED BY MEN AND WOMEN IN ANIMAL HUSBANDRY (DISTRICT BUDGAM)

Sl.No.	*Name of Activities*	*Mainly Done by Women*		*Mainly Done by Men*		*Both Response of*	
		Men	*Women*	*Men*	*Women*	*Men*	*Women*
1.	Cleaning sheds	09	23	05	17	03	40
2.	Preparing feed	07	21	08	16	02	43
3.	Buying feed	02	19	13	57	02	04
4.	Giving feed	07	31	29	09	02	20
5.	Giving water	08	39	08	13	01	20
6.	Milking	13	47	02	01	02	32
7.	Shearing	10	51	05	09	02	20
8.	Grazing	02	10	13	43	02	27
9.	Caring for sick animals	01	35	02	04	14	44
10.	Deciding to buy/sell animals	00	07	11	61	06	12
11.	Processing milk products	11	39	04	19	02	12
12.	Processing wool	00	00	15	75	02	05
13.	Selling milk	06	19	08	47	03	14

performed by men, while less labour intensive, but more time consuming activities are taken care of by women.

The traditional belief that women should not perform economic activities outside their homes has faded away even in rural areas in Kashmir. Moreover, the favourable social ethos helped women to work outside their homes for economic purpose. This situation regarding the out-home economic role prevails at the ideational levels as well as at the empirical level and applies to all classes, castes and groups. Our investigation in Baramulla and Budgam districts showed that women perform some important economic activities outside their home for economic purpose. Table 6.6 shows reply in response to a pointed question regarding the economic role of women outside their families.

TABLE 6.6

SHOULD WOMEN WORK OUTSIDE FOR EARING MONEY

Sl.No.	*Response*	*Baramulla Response of*		*Budgam Response of*		*Total*
		Men	*Women*	*Men*	*women*	
1.	Yes	67	103	88	53	311
2.	No	33	47	12	97	189
	Total	100	150	100	150	500

Table 6.6 reveals that a dominant majority of respondents, i.e., 311/500 (62.20 per cent), opined that women should work outside their homes for economic purpose. These respondents composed of 156 women and 155 men. At the same time, 189/500 (37.80 per cent) respondents were not in favour of women's activities outside their homes for economic purpose. These respondents included 45 men and 144 women. These two responses reveal three specific points. First, an overhelming majority of women favour their economic role outside their homes on remunerative basis. Second, more women than men like women's out-home economic activities by women. Third, refusal to allow women to work outside their homes comes mainly from the conservative religious forces, though this criticism (of women's broader role) loses relevance day by day.

The dominant response to the question of favouring women to work indicates two particular points. First, women must work outside their homes. Second, women must work on remunerative basis. These responses can be explained in terms of the broader and deeper impact of education, mass media, urbanization and rising costs of standard of life. Moreover, women prefer to work outside their homes because it keeps them busy during the daytime and supports them economically.

As is clear from the preceding section, women in rural areas here have opted for the adoption of working role outside their homes and on remunerative basis. However, these women have different preferences for the work they intend to perform. In our inquiry in Baramulla and Budgam districts, men and women respondents have shown preferences for working in different fields as shown in Tables 6.7 and 6.8.

While Table 6.7 portrays the picture which prevails at present in the villages of these districts, the latter table shows the views of respondents regarding their choice to work outside their homes on remunerative basis. In fact, these two tables reveal not so different responses and priorities for women's work in different economic fields. There stands coherence in the responses at serial nos. 1, 2, 4, 8, 12 (Tables 6.7 and 6.8). There seems certain degree of co-relation between the responses shown in these two tables. We are also in a position to establish priorities of the respondents regarding women's work based on the following rating:

(i) governmental service

(ii) family farming

(iii) shawl embroidery

(iv) preparing handicraft items

(v) work in orchards

(vi) dairy work

(vii) carpet weaving

(viii) trade

TABLE 6.7

WORKS DONE BY WOMEN FOR EARNING MONEY

Sl.No.	District	Baramulla		Budgam		
	Name of Work	Men	Women	Men	Women	Total
1.	Family farming	56	125	98	35	344
2.	Dairy	40	60	17	80	197
3.	Sheep rearing	16	15	47	25	103
4.	Work in orchards	45	55	51	37	188
5.	Wage labour in agriculture	04	40	00	08	52
6.	Wage labour in orchards	07	15	03	18	43
7.	Wage labour in carpet weaving	25	30	17	35	107
8.	Wage labour in shawl embroidery	20	95	21	55	191
9.	Producing handicraft items	12	35	12	15	74
10.	Trade	00	00	00	00	00
11.	Other wage labour	00	00	00	00	00
12.	Service/salary	30	41	41	21	133
13.	Others	00	00	00	00	00

TABLE 6.8

NATURE OF WORKS WOMEN SHOULD DO TO EARN MONEY

Sl.No.	*District*	*Baramulla*		*Budgam*		
	Name of Work	*Men*	*Women*	*Men*	*Women*	*Total*
1.	Family farming	43	85	71	14	213
2.	Dairy	12	41	45	05	103
3.	Sheep rearing	06	03	07	00	16
4.	Work in orchards	10	43	52	12	117
5.	Wage labour in agriculture	00	06	00	00	06
6.	Wage labour in orchards	00	13	04	04	21
7.	Wage labour in carpet weaving	12	60	15	16	49
8.	Wage labour in shawl embroidery	41	75	17	06	139
9.	Producing handicraft items	37	60	11	41	149
10.	Trade	04	13	12	12	42
11.	Other wage labour	00	00	00	00	00
12.	Service/salary	47	91	45	41	224
13.	Others	Nil	Nil	Nil	Nil	Nil

(ix) sheep rearing

(x) agricultural labour

There was no response which favoured women's work as wage labour except in agriculture.

Though, there was a dominant response in favour of women's economic activities, a tiny minority of respondents opposed it. Our investigation showed following categories of reasons for this particular response:

(i) economic reasons cited by 01.02 per cent respondents.

(ii) cultural and social reasons cited by 35.00 per cent respondents.

(iii) religious reasons cited by 01.00 per cent respondents.

The control over different types of assets is very important and this helps in knowing the authority of a person in certain fields. This possession also determines the status of a person in broader society. In order to know the ideal and real position of women within and outside their families, a question about their control over moveable and immoveable assets was asked. The response received has been recorded in Tables 6.9 and 6.10.

The above tables reveal the patterns of response as under:

- Animals control is with men and should remain with men.
- Agricultural land should be with men. Not a single respondent favoured that its ownership should remain with women.
- Cash is with sexes and should remain so. No respondent feels that it should be in the exclusive control of one sex.
- Control on radio (and television) should remain with both sexes.
- Control on jewellery is with sexes, but most of the respondents favoured its control to be with women. Not a single respondent agreed with its control with the males exclusively.

TABLE 6.9

CONTROL ON ASSETS BY MEN AND WOMEN (DISTRICT BARAMULLA)

Sl. No.	Assets	Control at Present With						Should have Control With					
		Men		Women		Both		Men		Women		Both	
		Response of		Response of		Response of		Responses of		Response of		Response of	
		Men	Women	Men	Women	Men	Women	Men	Women	Men	Women	Men	Women
1.	Animals	60	97	11	04	29	49	47	35	00	13	53	102
2.	Agriculture land	57	123	00	00	43	27	63	26	00	00	37	124
3.	Cash	74	71	05	05	21	74	27	19	00	00	73	131
4.	Radio	46	80	04	00	50	70	16	26	00	00	84	126
5.	Jewellery	06	12	57	105	37	33	00	00	69	89	31	61

TABLE 6.10

CONTROL ON ASSETS BY MEN AND WOMEN (DISTRICT BUDGAM)

Sl. No.	Assets	Control at Present With						Should have Control With					
		Men		Women		Both		Men		Women		Both	
		Response of		Response of		Response of		Response of		Response of		Response of	
		Men	*Women*	*Men*	*Women*	*Men*	*Women*	*Men*	*Women*	*Men*	*Women*	*Men*	*Women*
1.	Animals	37	83	12	00	51	67	35	40	00	14	65	96
2.	Agriculture land	47	98	00	05	53	47	41	02	00	10	56	138
3.	Cash	93	78	00	13	07	59	37	08	00	07	63	135
4.	Radio	90	108	00	03	10	41	00	74	00	06	100	70
5.	Jewellery	00	47	89	27	11	09	00	00	97	138	12	61

The nature of decision-making within and outside families reflects the status of persons concerned in the broader society. This also affects the gender bias in in-family and out-family situations. In order to know the reality in this regard in Baramulla and Budgam districts, a particular question was asked about actual decision-making and desired decision-making on the part of men and women or both. The response has been recorded in the Tables 6.11 and 6.12.

Tables 6.11 and 6.12 convey following pattern/s of decision-making on the part of men and women within their families:

- ***Sale and Purchase of Land:*** The relevant decisions are taken by men and both sexes and desired to be taken by both sexes. Not a single respondent favoured women's sole decision-making in this regard.
- ***Sale of crop/food items:*** The relevant decisions are taken mainly by men and both sexes and are desired to be taken by both sexes.
- ***Sale and Purchase of Animals :*** These decisions are taken mainly by men and are desired to be taken by both sexes.
- ***Sale of Animal Products;*** These decisions are taken by men and both sexes and these decisions should be taken by both sexes.
- ***Size of Family :*** The relevant decision is taken by both sexes and men, and this decision should be taken by both sexes. There was very less reponse in favour of this decision being taken by women or men alone.

* ***Education of Children:*** This decision is taken by both sexes and should be taken by both.
* ***Treatment of Son and Daughter:*** Decision in this regard is taken by men and should be taken by both men and women.
* ***Marriage of Children:*** This decision is taken by both, men and women and this practice must be maintained. However, men have developed an upper hand in this decision-making.

The above responses reflect a significant degree of change in the traditional situation related to decision-making on broader

TABLE 6.11

DECISION-MAKING IN THE FAMILY (BUDGAM DISTRICT)

Sl. No.	Name of Diff. Activities	Decision making of diff. activities at present						Desired change in decision made					
		Men Response of		Women Response of		Both Response of		Men Responses of		Women Response of		Both Response of	
		Men	Women	Men	Women	Men	Women	Men	Women	Men	Women	Men	Women
1.	Sale and purchase of land	95	85	00	00	05	65	37	15	00	20	63	125
2.	Sale of crop of food	93	91	00	12	07	47	43	08	00	01	57	141
3.	Sale and purchase of animal	93	117	00	02	07	31	41	10	00	03	59	137
4.	Sale of animal products	91	125	00	12	09	13	31	"	00	"	69	"
5.	Size of the family	12	122	08	17	80	11	09	"	00	"	91	150
6.	Education of children	12	06	01	45	87	89	00	10	00	03	100	137
7.	Treatment of sons illness	17	12	00	39	83	99	10	51	00	09	90	90
8.	Treatment of daughters illness	00	"	00	"	100	"	"	"	"	"	"	"
9.	Marriage of children	00	46	00	23	100	81	00	03	"	06	100	141

TABLE 6.12
DECISION-MAKING IN THE FAMILY BARAMULLA DISTRICT

Sl. No.	Name of Diff. Activities	Decision making of diff. activities at present						Desired change in decision made					
		Men		Women		Both		Men		Women		Both	
		Response of		Response of		Response of		Responses of		Response of		Response of	
		Men	Women	Men	Women	Men	Women	Men	Women	Men	Women	Men	Women
1.	Sale and purchase of land	57	131	00	00	43	19	30	50	06	00	64	100
2.	Sale of crop or food	53	135	11	00	36	15	41	53	02	00	57	97
3.	Sale and purchase of animal	52	115	10	00	34	35	38	74	04	00	68	78
4.	Sale of animal products	"	113	"	00	"	37	59	60	00	00	41	90
5.	Size of the family	49	86	21	00	30	64	40	00	03	16	67	134
6.	Education of children	43	40	10	00	47	110	15	00	04	00	81	150
7.	Treatment of sons illness	41	08	06	00	53	142	20	00	05	00	75	150
8.	Treatment of daughters illness	"	06	"	00	"	144	"	00	"	00	"	150
9.	Marriage of children	25	13	14	00	61	137	25	00	04	00	81	150

and basic issues and problems. It seems that a consensus has emerged or is emerging fast according to which all crucial and major decisions in the family are taken jointly by men and women.

The state and central governments introduced several programmes/schemes to help the people in rural areas. Most of these programmes/schemes are directed towards women to help them especially in the areas of health, nutrition, income, education, mobility and so on. These programmes/schemes have influenced the concerned segments of women in Baramulla and Budgam districts in Kashmir. In our investigation, a dominant majority of respondents felt that they were affected by various programmes/schemes. But, at the same time, they upheld that they were not benefited significantly. Moreover, significant number of respondents were not aware about various programmes/schemes and the facilities provided under them.

Our investigation revealed that a significant number of respondents were aware about uses of the policies of the government. However, it seems that a good number of people have not been benefited fully by these governmental programmes/schemes. We found that out of 300 women respondents in Baramulla and Budgam districts, 53 (i.e. 17.60 per cent) recalled spontaneously when asked about IRDP. At the same time, 39/300 (13.00 per cent) respondents recalled the programme after being aided by some people. We also found that Aanganwadi scheme was most popular government scheme in these districts. A dominant number of respondents (i.e. 222/300, 74.00 per cent) knew about this scheme and responded spontaneously when asked about it. A good number of them (i.e. 83/300, 24.60 per cent) knew about the utilization and use of the scheme also. A small number of respondents knew little about schemes like DWCRA and TRYSEM. This may be correct even if they are being benefited by these schemes. The information gathered during fieldwork revealed that programmes of loans and trainings are also not known to the people, though they may be benefited by them. It is mainly because no proper and relevant publicity about these programmes was carried out.

7

FINDINGS : HEALTH CONDITIONS IN KASHMIRI SOCIETY

Sound health stands as one of the primary conditions for a normal and prosperous society. It is also necessary for the continuity and growth of society. The health system becomes operational and effective by making its facilities available to every individual free of cost or on lesser cost. This seems correct in the case of developed societies and more correct in the case of developing countries. In addition to many other aspects, the health status of men and women reflects important dimension/s related to gender discrimination in the broader society. It follows that if the availability of medical facilities to men and women are disproportionate, the degree of gender discrimination may be high. On the other hand, if the availability of medical facilities (and their utilization) to men and women is equal or near-to-equal, the degree of gender discrimination may be low. In this context, it may be argued that availability and utilization of medical facilities by men and women are directly related to (and reflect the pattern of) gender discrimination in the broader society.

All above-mentioned propositions can be applied to the relevant situation prevailing in the Kashmir valley. In actuality, women face more medical problems than their male counterparts. It is primarily because they face crucial and dangerous health problems, especially before and after the delivery of child/children. Moreover, they are not provided proper and highly-needed treatment at the pre-natal and post-natal stages. Thus, all required medical facilities are not provided to them, especially in the rural areas. Women also do not avail all facilities which are provided to them. This is partly because of their ignorance about these facilities and partly because of the apathetic attitude on the part of the medical staff and administration. Among other things, this medical situation reflects a set pattern of gender discrimination. The male-dominated medical staff and administration introduce and maintain certain degree of male bias in providing medical facilities. These aspects of gender discrimination reveal clearly in the following findings:

During our investigation in Baramulla and Budgam districts, we enquired about the health status of women respondents. In response, we came across some of the important aspects of the health of women. We asked a particular question about the birth of child/children in her/their families and their survival in last two years. In this respect, we got the response entered in Table 7.1

TABLE 7.I

NUMBER OF CHILDREN BORN IN THE FAMILY

Sl. No.	*How many children were Born in your Family during last Two Years*	*Baramulla district*	*Budgam district*	*Total*	
				No.	*Percentage*
1	Yes	55	43	98	32.40
2.	No	95	107	202	67.30
	Total	150	150	300	100

Table 7.1 reveals that in majority of the cases, i.e., 202 out of 300 (67.30 per cent), there was no birth in their families during the last two years. On the other hand, there were some (01-03) births in the families in the case of 98 out of 300 (32.60 per cent) respondents. These two types of information do not reveal the reality and totality of the actual births in Baramulla and Budgam districts, but we may infer two important points in this regard. First, there have been (comparatively) lesser births in these districts in two previous years. This lower birth rate can be associated with (among other factors) successful family planning programmes in these districts. Second, respondents didn't convey correct information or made attempts to hide the

correct information mainly due to the reasons related to militancy.

Another important question, related to availability/utilization of relevant health facilities during the period of pregnancy in last two years, was posed to the respondents, especially to those who were pregnant. We got the response which portrays in Table 7.2.

TABLE 7.2

HEALTH FACILITES UTILIZED DURING THE PERIOD OF PREGNANCY

Sl. No.	*Did she (who gave birth) avail any health service?*	*District Baramulla*	*District Budgam*	*Total*	
				Number	*Percentage*
1.	Yes	35	40	75	76.2
2.	No	10	x	10	10.6
3.	Cannot say	10	03	13	13.2
	Total	55	43	98	100

Table 7.2 reveals clearly that a significant number of respondents, i.e., 75/98 (76.20 per cent), availed the relevant health facilities provided by the government by themselves or their nearest relatives, while 10/98 (i.e., 10.60 per cent) respondents did not avail at all any such facility available at the district level health centres/hospitals. The rest of the respondents, i.e., 13/98 (13.2 per cent), did not show any response to this question. The preceding responses can be explained in the following ways. First, most of the medical facilities, especially related to the pregnancy, availed by the respondents were mostly located in the city of Srinagar and not at the tehsil or block level. Most of the towns in Baramulla and Budgam districts, like other districts in the valley, lacked most of these medical facilities. Second, those who could not avail relevant medical facilities in two districts belonged to the villages where such facilities are not available. They were also not in a position to come to Srinagar for availing such facilities. They had to depend either on meagre medical facilities available at the tehsil or block level or on traditional medical practices. Third, those who did not avail were in fact those who could not avail medical facilities. This was partly because of non-availability of

medical facilities at tehsil-village level and partly because of disturbed conditions due to the militancy-related activities. Fourth, the most important point is that degree of authenticity and reliability may be low. It is because the entire medical system was disturbed due to militancy. Even if the medical facilities were available, these could not be utilized in the disturbed situation. In some cases, even the village-tehsil level health centres were destroyed or the medical/para-medical staff was not allowed to work normally and regularly.

We also enquired from our respondents in Baramulla and Budgam districts about their experience related to abortion in their family/families during two previous years. Their response is shown in Table 7.3

TABLE 7.3

NUMBER OF ABORTIONS OF THE WOMEN

Sl. No.	*Abortion you had*	*District Baramulla*	*District Budgam*	*Total*	
				Number	*Percentage*
1.	Yes	12	08	20	6.60
2.	No	138	142	280	93.40
	Total	150	150	300	100

The preceding table divulges that while 20 out of 300 respondents (6.60 per cent) have undergone abortion in various health centres in the Kashmir valley for health/medical reasons, 280 out of 300 (93.40 per cent) respondents had no such experience. In the light of experience in the Kashmir valley, this response seems unrealistic. This can be explained further by the following reasons. First, majority of the respondents (who have undergone abortions) never reveal that they have undergone such experience partly because this act does not enjoy religious and social approval in the traditional Kashmiri society and partly because of direct or indirect threat of the militants who openly abhor this practice. Second, the official figures hide rather than reveal the actual situation. It is more so in a situation in which the decadal census of 1991, was not carried out. Third, the religious-oriented militant movement in Kashmir had negated even the concept of abortion, though Islam has allowed this act when it is necessary for saving the child or woman. In that situation, most of the people, especially women, who wanted to undergo abortion for family planning purpose, carried out this act outside the state, particularly in Jammu, Delhi and Chandigarh. These abortions could neither be reported to the general public nor recorded by the concerned official agencies.

In order to know about the child mortality rate, we enquired from our respondents whether all their children were alive after their birth or not. As is common in Kashmir, all children who are born do not survive after their birth. There can be many reasons for their death. Lack of basic / primary medical facilities or not availing of even meagre available medical facilities can also be considered as one of the major causes of death. Our investigation in this regard and the consequent response is given in the following table.

TABLE 7.4

NUMBER OF CHILDREN SURVIVED AFTER BIRTH

Sl.No.	*Are all Children Alive/*	*District Baramulla*	*District Budgam*	*Total Number*	*Total Percentage*
1.	Yes	130	139	269	90
2.	No	13	08	21	07
3.	No	07	03	10	03
	Total	150	150	300	100

Table 7.4 shows that highest number of children survived after their birth. The research reveals that 269 out of 300 (90.00 per cent) respondents remained alive after their birth. Though this figure does not seem realistic, it essentially points to the aspect of utilization of medical and non-medical facilities, mainly at the non-Government level, on the part of concerned women in district headquarters or cities within and outside Kashmir. It was also observed that most of these respondents had gone to Srinagar, Jammu and other cities in northern India for their own or relative women's delivery. On the other hand, only 21/300 (7.00 per cent) respondents conveyed that their children did not survive after their birth mainly because minimum health/ medical facilities were not available in their villages and tehsils. These children belonged mainly to the 0-5 years age group

and were from both sexes. This response too does not seem realistic because it hides the actual situation. We are not in a position to confirm or reject these figures in the absence of relevant census data of 1991, or after that. However, the overall situation reflect not a grim picture of gender discrimination *vis-a-vis* health/medical facilities.

We made an important query from the female respondents who had given birth to a child or children during the period of last two years. It was about the use of necessary drugs such as iron tablets, tetnus toxoid, and so on, before the delivery of the child or children. In response to this question, we got the information which has been included in Table 7.5.

TABLE 7.5

MEDICINES USED BY WOMEN DURING PREGNANCY

Sl.No.	*Did you take Tetnus Toxoid/ Iron tab during Pregnancy?*	*Tetnus Toxoid*		*Iron Tablets*	
		Baramulla	*Budgam*	*Baramulla*	*Budgam*
1.	Yes	41	34	41	34
2.	No	14	09	14	09
	Total	55	43	55	43

Table 7.5 reveals that not a very insignificant number of respondents, who were all women, used above-mentioned drugs during the period of their pregnancy. All of them usually belonged to higher-middle income and educated groups. Moreover, they had close and strong family contact in Srinagar and other cities outside the J & K state. It is important to note that this response was collected in the period when militancy was strong in these districts and all Primary Health Centres and other health-care centres were completely non-functional. Thus, the respondents who used drugs had to go to cities within and outside Kashmir.

During our investigation, we also enquired from the female respondents about the place of birth of their children in last two years time. This has been shown in Table 7.6.

TABLE 7.6

PLACE OF BIRTH OF CHILDREN OF THE RESPONDENTS

Sl.No.	*Birth took place at*	*Baramulla*	*Budgam*	*Total No.*	*Percentage*
1.	Home	24	11	35	34.3
2.	Government Hospital	23	15	38	37.2
3.	Private Hospital	8	17	25	28.5
	Total	55	43	98	100

Table 7.6 reveals that in majority of the cases, the delivery of children took place either in the respondents homes or in private clinics. These private clinics include the residences of some doctors who usually go for private practice before or after their hospital work. Our respondents revealed that 35 out of 98 (34.30 per cent) women delivered their babies at their own homes. This may be explained in terms of the militancy situation in which it was highly risky even to go out of the villages. On the other hand, 38/98 and 25/98 women gave birth to their babies in government hospitals and private hospitals respectively.

Research was also carried out about the role of a person who conducted the delivery of children. This has been given in Table 7.7.

TABLE 7.7

CONDUCT OF DELIVERY OF CHILDREN

S.No.	*Delivery was Conducted by*	*District Baramulla*	*District Budgam*	*Total*	
				Number	*Percentage*
1.	Dai	21	11	32	32.6
2.	ANM	17	10	2.7	26.6
3.	Doctor	17	22	39	44.8
	Total	55	43	98	100

8

FINDINGS : ISSUES RELATED TO MARRIAGE

As has been observed in other societies / communities in the Indian sub-continent, the customary practice of dowry (given by the bride's family to the bridegroom's family) is also in vogue in the Kashmiri society in urban as well as rural areas. In fact, it stands as one of the important and common practices related to marriage. Our inquiry in this regard in two districts of Baramulla and Budgam revealed as is shown in Table 8.1.

TABLE 8.1

PAYMENT OF DOWRY AT THE TIME OF MARRIAGE OF GIRLS

Sl. No	*Is Dowry given to Girls ?*	*Baramulla*		*Budgam*		*Total*	
		Men	*Women*	*Men*	*Women*	*Number*	*Percentage*
1.	Yes	84	124	94	109	411	82
2.	No	08	20	00	10	38	18
3.	Cannot say	100	150	100	150	500	100

Table 8.1 reveals that dominant majority of respondents, i.e., 411 out of 500 (82.00 per cent), conveyed that they or their families have paid or will pay dowry at the time of marriage of their daughters/girls in their families. On the other hand, a tiny minority of 38 out of 500 (18.00 per cent) respondents did not pay or will not pay dowry at the time of marriage of their daughters/girls. It is interesting to note here that the dowry has not emerged as a dangerous problem for the girls and their parents. In actuality, the number of dowry deaths is very negligible in the valley. While the phenomenon of 'dowry demand' on the part of boy's family seems virtually absent, the phenomenon of 'voluntary dowry' on the part of girl's family

exists in most of the cases. In the latter case, the girls take a lot of things to the bridegroom's house with their consent. It has also been observed that the payment of dowry leads to more adjustment and stability of relations in the girl's in-laws family. In contrast, the non-payment of dowry contributes, among other factors, to more maladjustment and conflict in the girl's in-laws family.

Payment of Mehr

Payment of *Mehr* is considered another important issue for the women in Kashmir. It is felt that, at the time of marriage, the man agrees in writing to pay certain amount of money to the woman at the time or after the marriage. But, the common practice is that this amount is paid neither at the time or after the marriage. In some cases, *Mehr* in part is paid at the time of marriage and the rest is never paid. It emerges as crucial problem when the man divorces his wife and refuses to pay full amount of *Mehr.* (This perception has been presented by the framers of the questionnaire). It may not be out of place to mention here that, as per the Islamic injunctions, the man has to full amount of *Mehr* at the time of formalizing the *Nikah.*

The amount of *Mehr,* to be paid by a man to a woman at the time of marriage, is determined by the representatives of both parties according to the economic standard of the man. In actuality, there prevail differences in the amounts of *Mehr* paid by members of different classes, groups and communities. On the basis of information gathered in Baramulla and Budgam districts, we can categorize our respondents in three groups which paid three different amounts of *Mehr.* The details in this regard follow:

(i) 3000 - 9000 Lower income groups (composing of small farmers and landless labourers)

(ii) 10000 - 30000 Middle - Class groups (groups of small farmers and service classes)

(iii) 31000 - 50000 Upper middle - classes (small business groups and upper service classes) and

(iv)	51000 and above.	Upper classes (especially big businessmen).

As was mentioned earlier, the *Mehr* become a crucial problem in case the man refuses to pay the amount (of *Mehr*) at the time of divorce. Our inquiry in this field revealed the information included in Table 8.2.

Table 8.2 reveals that a majority of 306 out of 500 (i.e., 61.20 per cent) respondents felt that the amount of *Mehr* decided at the *Nikah* time was paid either at the time of *Nikah* or divorce. Among these 306 respondents, majority got full or part of the amount at the time of *nikah* and the remaining not receiving the deferred amount. In actuality, in the stable or harmonious environment in the family, could hardly demand this amount. On the other hand, 194 out of 500 38.80 per cent respondents conveyed that the pre-decided amount of *mehr* was neither paid fully at the time of *nikah* nor paid at the time of divorce. The respondents held that, as per the customary practices in the rural areas of Kashmir, the pre-decided amount was never paid to the woman fully either at the time of *nikah* or divorce. They also felt that this practice stood clearly against the injunctions of Islam.

Divorce to Women

Usually, the practice of divorce is abhorred by Kashmiris and this practice stands completely undesirable in their society. So, the incidence of divorce in the Kashmir valley is very less. Our investigation in this regard in the districts of Baramulla and Budgam gave the information shown in Table 8.3 .

Table 8.3 shows that very less number of respondents, i.e., 40 out of 500 (10.00 per cent), reported that there have been lesser incidences of divorce in their families. On the contrary, the dominant majority of respondents, i.e., 403 out of 500 (80.60 per cent) reported that they have not experienced any divorce in their families. This response was supported by the argument that the act of divorce on the part of men was highly disapproved and was considered extremely undersirable. Although there have been some lesser number of divorces, the practice in itself was not appreciated in any way in the entire Kashmir valley.

TABLE 8.2

PAYMENT OF MEHR AT THE TIME OF DIVORCE

Sl. No.	*Is payment of Mehr made at the time of Divorce?*	*District Buramulla*		*District Budgam*		*Total*	
		Men	*Women*	*Men*	*Women*	*Number*	*Percentage*
1.	Yes	74	98	51	83	306	61.2
2	No	26	52	49	67	194	38.8
	Total	100	150	100	150	500	100

TABLE 8.3

INCIDENCE OF DIVORCES

Sl. No.	Is there any incident of Divorce in your family?	Buramulla		Budgam		Total	
		Men	Women	Men	Women	Number	Percentage
1.	Yes	07	21	08	14	50	10
2.	No	93	94	92	124	403	80.6
3.	Cannot say	00	35	00	12	47	9.4
	Total	100	150	100	150	500	100

Among other factors, the community intervention to stop all possibilities of practising divorce is responsible for this situation.

Remarriage of Divorcees and Widows

After getting divorces, the Muslim women in the Kashmir valley, like in other Muslim communities, get married and it is not considered a taboo. Our research in this field gave us the information included in Table 8.4.

TABLE 8.4

REMARRIAGE OF DIVORCEES AND WIDOWS

Sl. No.	*Are the parties Concerned married*	*District Baramulla*	*District Budgam*	*Total*	
				Number	*Percentage*
1.	Husband married	13	17	30	30
2.	Wife married	06	08	14	44
3.	None married	21	09	30	30
4.	Do not Know	16	10	26	26
	Total	56	44	100	100

Table 8.3 revealed that there occured 50 cases of divorce in the families of our respondents. This follows that 100 people (women as well as men) in total were affected on both sides in this situation. These people included 56 persons (28 persons from each sex) from Baramulla district and 44 persons (22 persons from each sex) from Budgam district. However, Table 8.4 reveals that 30 men out of total 100 divorced were remarried, while 14 women out of total 100 divorced were remarried. Similarly, the investigation conveyed that 30 persons out of this lot had not remarried, while there was no information available about 10 persons. This data reflects the concerned empirical reality prevailing in the Kashmiri society. The explanation follows. First, while divorce is considered undesirable, its practice, at the same time, is not treated as taboo. In fact, the divorce does not make a woman an untouchable. Second, usually both men and women divorcees remarry or at least intend to marry again. The remarriage of men and women depends, among other factors, on the number and age of children at the time of divorce, economic situation of the persons involved, educational and social status of the persons involved and family background.

Another important and related question asked to the respondents was about remarriage of persons involved of both sexes after their divorces. The information collected in this regard, has been shown in the Tables 8.5 and 8.6.

Tables 8.5 and 8.6 convey that 59.20 per cent (296 out of 500) respondents said 'yes' in response to the question posed to them (if it was easy for men to remarry after divorce?). On the other hand, 40.80 per cent (204 out of 500) respondents answered in the negative to this question. While the former response can be explained in terms of the positive chances of men's remarriage in the marriage market, the latter response hints towards the crucial problems which emerge for a man to marry after divorce. At the same time, the preceding response was in total contrast to the response which came from the divorced women. In their case, the dominant majority among them, i.e., 263 out of 500 (52.60 per cent), did not marry after their divorces. While a lesser number of respondents, i.e., 75 out of 500 (15.00 per cent), said 'yes' to this question. A significant number of respondents, i.e., 162 out of 500 (32.40 per cent), remained silent in response to this question.

In this survey, we made an inquiry about the specific reasons for which women got divorces from their husbands. The respondents' response revealed two set of reasons, one given by men and other by women. The reasons given by the men respondents include the following:

(i) Husband's immorality;

(ii) Sexual problems;

(iii) Denial of authority to women;

(iv) Dowry demands on the part of in-laws family;

(v) Misunderstanding between husband and wife;

(vi) Conflict between the wife and husband;

(vii) Non-fulfillment of women's needs;

(viii) Beating of wives;

(ix) Ugly features of the husband/wife; and

(x) Non-earning status of the wife.

TABLE 8.5
REMARRIAGE OF MEN AFTER DIVORCES

Sl. No.	*Is it Easy for a Man to Remarry after Divorce ?*	*Buramulla*		*Budgam*		*Total*	
		Men	*Women*	*Men*	*Women*	*Number*	*Percentage*
1.	Yes	61	94	21	120	296	59.2
2.	No	39	56	79	30	204	40.8
	Total	100	150	100	150	500	100

TABLE 8.6

REMARRIAGE OF WOMEN AFTER DIVORCES

Sl. No	Is it Easy for Women to get Remarried after Divorce?	Baramulla		Budgam		Total	
		Men	Women	Men	Women	Number	Percentage
1.	Yes	06	57	00	12	75	15
2.	No	61	37	91	74	263	52.6
3.	Cannot say	33	56	09	64	162	32.4
	Total	100	150	100	150	500	100

On the other hand, the reasons given by women respondents included the following:

(i) Ignoring the women's basic needs;

(ii) Sexual problems;

(iii) Misunderstanding between husband and wife;

(iv) Forced marriage;

(v) Bad character of the husband;

(vi) No adjustment in in-laws family;

(vii) Family-marital disputes;

(viii) Cronic diseases;

(ix) Consumption of drugs and liquor and

(x) Wife-beating.

The women in Kashmir generally remarry after their husbands' death. This applies to all areas, classes, groups and communities. In this context, we attempted to know the basic attitudes of men and women towards the remarriage of widows. Our question in this connection got the response which reflects in Table 8.7.

Table 8.7 shows that an overwhelming majority of respondents, i.e., 387 out of 500 (77.40 per cent) were in favour of remarriage of women after the death of their husbands. There are 33 out of 500 (06.60 per cent) respondents who opined that the widows should not marry again at all. The former response can be related to several factors. The most important factor is the religion of Islam (which is practised by 97.00 per cent people in the Kashmir valley) which allows as well as emphasizes the marriage of women even after the death of their husbands. The other factor of equal importance is the impact of the processes of modernization, especially of modern education, mass media, cultural exposure and economic prosperity.

More or less similar attitudes were found among the respondents regarding men's remarriage after the death of their wives. The question in this regard attracted the respondents response as is mentioned in the Table 8.8

TABLE 8.7

REMARRIAGE OF WOMEN AFTER DEATH OF THEIR HUSBANDS

Sl. No.	*Should women marry after her husband's death ?*	*Buramulla*		*Budgam*		*Total*	
		Men	*Women*	*Men*	*Women*	*Number*	*Percentage*
1.	Yes	71	110	91	115	387	77.4
2.	No	00	05	03	25	33	66
3.	Cannot say	29	35	06	10	80	16
	Total	100	150	100	150	500	100

TABLE 8.8

REMARRIAGE OF MEN AFTER DEATH OF THEIR WIVES

Sl. No.	*Should a men marry re-marry after wife's death ?*	*Buramulla*		*Budgam*		*Total*	
		Men	*Women*	*Men*	*Women*	*Number*	*Percentage*
1.	Yes	81	105	98	122	406	81.2
2.	No	11	10	02	28	51	10.2
3.	Can not say	08	35	00	00	43	8.6
	Total	100	150	100	150	500	100

Table 8.8 reveals that the dominant majority of respondents, i.e. 406 out of 500 (81.20 per cent), were in favour of remarriage of men whose wives have died due to any reason. On the other hand, 10.20 (out of 500) per cent respondents favoured no marriage for men whose wives have passed away due to any reason. While the former response can be explained in terms of factors referred in the preceding case, the latter response is shown because of various problems which this type of marriage creates for the children of the earlier couple, especially in the fields of inheritance rights, maladjustment, discrimination, psychological depression and normal growth. These reasons can also be related to the second response in the preceding table.

An important inquiry was made during the investigation about the residence of widows. The response we got in this regard has been entered in Table 8.9.

In general, divorce is allowed but, at the same time, considered an undesirable practice in the Kashmir valley. In reality, the right of divorce is practised by a male person as the last resort formalizing the separation between husband and wife. In this broader context, we enquired from the respondents whether it is easy for a male person to divorce his wife ? Then we asked this question in other way, i.e., is it easy for female person to get divorce from her husband? The response to these questions we got is portrayed in Tables 8.10 and 8.11.

Table 8.10 reveals that 273 out of 500 (54.60 per cent) respondents in Baramulla and Budgam districts are of the opinion that divorce/s on the part of husbands stand as an easy affair, while the rest 227 out of 500 (45.40 per cent) respondents believed that it is not an easy affair, while the former type of response reveals the legal aspect of divorce, i.e., a male person can easily, though on sound reason, divorce his wife, the latter type of response conveys the social, economic, psychological and other aspects related to the divorce. In the latter case, it emerges as a complex and not a simple, phenomenon in the society. It gives rise to lot many problems to the women, children and families concerned.

TABLE 8.9
REMARRIAGE OF WIDOWS AFTER DEATH OF THEIR HUSBANDS

Sl. No.	*Women Stay after the Death of their Husband With*	*Baramulla*		*Budgam*		*Total*	
		Men	*Women*	*Men*	*Women*	*Number*	*Percentage*
1.	Husband's family	90	137	89	97	413	82.6
2.	Her natal family	10	10	11	44	75	15
3.	On her own	00	03	00	09	12	2.4
4.	Others	00	00	00	00	00	00
	Total	100	150	100	150	500	100

TABLE 8.10

IS IT EASY FOR A HUSBAND TO DIVORCE HIS WIFE

Sl. No.	*Is it easy for a man to Divoce his wife ?*	*Baramulla*		*Budgam*		*Total*	
		Men	*Women*	*Men*	*Women*	*Number*	*Percentage*
1.	Yes	61	79	38	95	273	54.6
2.	No	39	71	62	55	227	45.4
	Total	100	150	100	150	500	100

TABLE 8.11

IS IT EASY FOR A WIFE TO GET DIVORCE FROM HER HUSBAND

Sl. No.	*Is it easy for a women to get a Divorce ?*	*Buramulla*		*Budgam*		*Total*	
		Men	*Women*	*Men*	*Women*	*Number*	*Percentage*
1.	Yes	05	13	13	11	42	8.2
2.	No	55	107	50	112	324	64.8
3.	Cannot say	40	30	37	27	134	26
	Total	100	150	100	150	500	100

On the other hand, Table 8.11 conveys that it is not easy for a wife to get divorce in majority of the cases according to the views of respondents. Thus, 324 out of 500 (64.80 per cent) respondents expressed this opinion and held that this divorce created multifarious problems for them. Special mention was made about the problem in which they were not preferred as first wives (as compared to virgin women) in majority of the cases in the marriage market. This situation created other, rather multiplied their problems in their own and in-laws families after their second marriage. Table 8.11 also reveals that a tiny minority of 42 out of 500 (08.20 per cent) respondents maintained that they did not face any serious problem in getting divorces from their husbands, so it was relatively easy for them. Most of them belonged to upper economic and educated and culturally exposed families.

It was crucial to know about the place of residence of women after they divorce. The response in this regard is portrayed in Table 8.12.

The responses in Table 8.12 show various types of residences adopted by the concerned women after divorces. The types of residences may be identified as follows :

(i) Dominant majority of respondents, 414 out of 500 (82.80 per cent) joined and lived with their natal families after getting divorce. This type of residence by the divorcees was justified by them by arguing that the natal family provides all kinds of security needed by them and their children.

(ii) A small number of 16 out of 500 (03.20 per cent) respondents lived separately but within the broader household of the former husband. The compulsion for this type of stay was that these women had nobody to take care of them, especially from their parental families.

(iii) An insignificant number of 60 out of 500 (12.00 per cent) respondents lived on their own by establishing a new household. Most of them were self-earning women.

Table 8.12 indicates three types of residences adopted by the widows immediately after the death of their husbands. The details in this regard follow :

TABLE 8.12
PLACE OF RESIDENCE OF DIVORCED WOMEN

Sl. No.	Divorced Women lives with	Baramulla		Budgam		Total	
		Men	Women	Men	Women	Number	Percentage
1.	Her husbands family	00	16	00	00	16	3.2
2.	Her natal family	71	129	87	127	414	82.8
3.	On her own	29	05	13	13	60	12
	Others	00	00	00	10	10	2
	Total	100	150	100	150	500	100

(i) 82.60 per cent (413 out of 500) respondents lived in their husbands' property ;

(ii) 15.00 per cent (75 out of 500) respondents lived in their natal/parental families till they remarried;

(iii) 02.40 per cent (12 out of 500) respondents established their new household unit and lived on their own resources.

It was observed that the divorced women in general work outside their homes and make their living honourable. This situation exists despite the fact that these (divorced) women are not neglected by their parental families or community in general. In our areas of research, the divorced women were working outside their homes in the following fields :

- Family farming;
- Wage labour in orchards;
- Producing various handicraft items ;
- Carpet weaving and blanket making and
- Government services.

Children's Support / Custody

The most crucial problem which emerged immediately after the formalities of divorce were over was directly related to the children's support and custody in the post-divorce period upto the time of their maturity. The important point in this regard is who has the right, legal or otherwise, after divorce takes place to keep and support the child/children. Our investigation among the respondents in this regard revealed the following aspects :

(i) Children mostly remain with their mothers, especially if they are too young to be taken care of by their fathers. In some cases, these children when they enter teens return to their fathers;

(ii) Occasionally, the children stay with mother for sometime and with father for sometime. The arrangement is usually predetermined;

(iii) If there are more than one child in the family, they can be divided among father and mother, with whom they stay for ever.

Another related problem which emerges in the post-divorce situation is the financial support to child/children which in ideal situation has to be borne by fathers. An enquiry among our respondents in this connection revealed the following patterns of financial support to children :

(i) It was reported that 65.00 per cent children were supported solely by their fathers for the entire period of childhood;

(ii) It was reported that 20.00 per cent children were supported financially by their fathers occasionally and not fully;

(iii) It was reported that 15.00 per cent children were not supported financially by their fathers at all. Consequently, mothers had to provide this support to the children.

An enquiry among our respondents was also made about the underlying reasons which compel or justify fathers' support to their children even after divorcing their wives. The reported categories of justifying reasons included the following:

(a) Children always depend on their fathers for financial support throughout their lives, especially upto the time they start earning themselves;

(b) Fathers also like to support financially their children, if they are in that position. They want to do this to keep constant contact with their children;

(c) Fathers want better care and upbringing for their children even if they live separately and even if fathers maintain their differences with their former wives;

(d) Fathers feel their responsibility to care of all needs of their children at least till they become majors. This feeling comes from moral, social and legal sources;

(e) Fathers feel the religious binding to provide total support, especially the financial, to their children even after they divorce their wives. It seems obligatory on their part.

The investigation was also carried out about the quantity of financial support to children by their fathers. It revealed that broadly there exist four major criteria on the basis of which the amount of support is fixed. These criteria are as follows:

(i) Fixation of the amount by senior/respected notables of the place;

(ii) On the basis of father's total income;

(iii) As per the essential/primary/total needs of children;

(iv) Children's choices and decisions.

Practice of Wife Beating

The practice of wife-beating is in vogue in all types of societies, rural, urban, traditional and modern. However, the practice stands more prone to rural areas in comparison to urban areas. In response to our investigation regarding this practice in the rural Kashmiri society, we got the information entered in Table 8.13.

Table 8.13 shows that while a significant number of respondents, i.e., 140 out of 500 (28.00 per cent), disclosed that people in their areas (which may include them also) beat their wives regularly in their villages/neighbourhood, 113 out of 500 (22.60 per cent) respondents gave the opposite response, i.e., wives are not beaten by their husbands.

Inheritance Rights

Women in Kashmir have a clear and definite share in their parents' and husbands' property according to the religious and customary laws. Since this aspect is of fundamental importance to the prevailing patterns of gender discrimination, we made a detailed inquiry in this connection. The first inquiry was made about whether women inherit from their parents property. The response in this regard is given in the Table 8.14.

Table 8.13 shows that majority of respondents, i.e., 327 out of 500 (65.40 per cent), conveyed that women do not inherit father's property partly or wholly, while 173 out of 500 (44.60 per cent) respondents agreed that they get the share in parental property. It was also conveyed by the respondents that the denial of certain share of women from their parental property stand in clear violation of the Islamic laws and moral, ethical and social rights of women.

TABLE 8.13
PREVELANCE OF THE PRACTICE OF WIFE BEATING

Sl. No.	*Do people beat their wives in your villages or neighbourhood?*	*Buramulla*		*Budgam*		*Total*	
		Men	*Women*	*Men*	*Women*	*Number*	*Percentage*
1.	Yes	35	45	29	31	140	28
2.	No	20	35	10	48	113	22.6
3.	Cannot say	45	70	61	71	247	49.4
	Total	100	150	100	150	500	100

TABLE 8.14

INHERITANCE BY WOMEN FROM THEIR PARENTS' PROPERTY

Sl. No.	*Do Women Inherit Father's property ?*	*Baramulla*		*Budgam*		*Total*	
		Men	*Women*	*Men*	*Women*	*Number*	*Percentage*
1.	Yes	45	80	21	27	173	34.6
2.	No	55	70	79	123	327	65.4
	Total	100	150	100	150	500	100

The share of females in their parental property stands lesser than their male counterparts, i.e., their brothers. This pattern of property distribution has number of reasons. First, they grow in their parents family and get their due share of parental property before or after their marriage. Second, they get certain share from their husband's property also. In this background, we enquired from our respondents about the amount of share of property of their parents. Their response is shown in Table 8.15.

Table 8.15 shows that an overwhelming majority of 95 per cent of respondents conveyed that women get lesser share than their brothers. This proportion/share of the parental property has been fixed by the Islamic Sharia. However, a tiny minority of 19 out of 500 (3.80 per cent) respondents conveyed that women get equal to brothers share. Both these responses of the respondents must be seen in the context of two crucial points. First, not many parents, especially in the rural areas, give to their share of property. Second, most of the respondents in our sample were not aware about due share of property from their parental property. It is essentially in this context that we can understand the response of women respondents in which some claimed to get 1/3 and others 2/3 from their parental property. However, during our fieldwork, we found that near-total women respondents were in favour of getting the exact share of parental property which their religion and Sharia has kept for them.

In all societies of the world, there prevails a certain specific opinion about the share of property of women in their parental and husband's property. Same is the case within the Kashmiri society. In order to know particular attitudes regarding women's share in their parental and other property in Kashmir, we sought the opinion of respondents during the investigation in Baramulla and Budgam districts. Table 8.16 gives the response of this investigation

Table 8.16 reveals different types of responses to the question regarding equal (with their brother) share of women as mentioned below:

TABLE 8.15

AMOUNT OF SHARE WOMEN GET FROM THEIR PARENTS PROPERTY

Sl. No	*Amt Women get as Compared to their Brothers?*	*Baramulla*		*Budgam*		*Total*	
		Men	*Women*	*Men*	*Women*	*Number*	*Percentage*
1.	Equal	00	01	11	07	19	3.8
2.	Less	100	149	89	137	475	95
3.	More	00	00	00	00	0	00
4.	No reply				06	6	1.2
	Total	100	150	100	150	500	100

TABLE 8.16

WOMEN'S SHARE IN THEIR PARENTS' PROPERTY

Sl. No.	*Should women get equal in Parental Property as their Brother?*	*Baramulla*		*Budgam*		*Total*	
		Men	*Women*	*Men*	*Women*	*Number*	*Percentage*
1.	Yes	45	37	12	70	164	32.8
2.	No	55	75	50	64	244	48.8
3.	Cannot say	00	38	38	16	92	18.4
	Total	100	150	100	150	500	100

(i) 164 out of 500 (32.80 per cent) respondents said that women should get equal share in parental property like their brothers.

(ii) 244 out of 500 (48.80 per cent) respondents should not get equal share (to that of their brother's) in their parental property.

(iii) 92 out of 500 (18.40 per cent) respondents did not express their opinion as the matter stands complex and controversial.

Women in general and widows in particular suffer in the field of inheritance rights in the parental and husbands' property. Though they may have some rights theoretically, but in practice they are denied these rights. In this context, we enquired specifically about the share of property which the widows get in rural Kashmir. The response we got is given in Table 8.17

Table 8.17 establishes the following patterns of inheriting the husband's property by the widows.

(i) 122 out of 500 (24.40 per cent) respondents felt that widows inherit always a particular share from their husbands' property.

(ii) 297 out of 500 (59.40 per cent) respondents felt that widows don't get a share from their husbands' property always. However, they get it sometimes depending upon the family situation.

(iii) 81 out of 500 (16.20 per cent respondents conveyed that the share of widows from their husbands' property is never given to them.

(iv) Majority of total respondents conveyed that the share of a widow from her husband's property is 1/8 in addition to his/her belongings. This, in fact, has been suggested by Islamic Sharia. Dominant majority of respondents observed that this 1/8 share is paid to widows in more or less all cases.

Family Disputes

The family disputes represent a usual phenomenon in all types of societies in the world. It has been observed that most

TABLE 8.17

INHERITANCE RIGHTS OF WIDOWS

Sl. No.	*Do widows inherit a share in their husbands property?*	*Baramulla*		*Budgam*		*Total*	
		Men	*Women*	*Men*	*Women*	*Number*	*Percentage*
1.	Always	30	65	12	15	122	24.4
2.	Sometimes	60	70	62	105	297	59.4
3.	Never	10	15	26	30	81	16.2
	Total	100	150	100	150	500	100

of these disputes revolve around claims and counterclaims of property. It has also been noticed that women in general suffer in these situation, partly because laws are not in their favour and partly because they cannot match the male muscle-power. When we enquired from our respondents in Baramulla and Budgam districts regarding the occurrence of family disputes, we received the information which reveals in Tables 8.18 and 8.19.

Table 8.18 shows that only 13.80 per cent of the total respondents approached the court / s in connection with family dispute revolving around property. Among these respondents, while 69.60 per cent women knocked the doors of the court/s for getting justice, 25.20 per cent men took the initiative of getting justice from the court/s. In rest of the cases, both men and women jointly approached the court with their claims and counter-claims.

It was observed during the investigation that most of the women were helped by their concerned men (especially by the primary kin) or were forced to go to the courts themselves. In actuality, women in Kashmir generally avoid to involve themselves in the court/s and prefer to resolve the family disputes through the intervention of home members, relatives, friends and neighbours. During the investigation, it revealed that some women respondents approached the community forums for resolving the family disputes. Thus, it reveals that courts have not developed enough approval among the rural women.

Temporary Migration

A good number of people from all parts of Kashmir, especially from rural areas, migrate to other parts of the state and country for working and earning money. This migration, of the cyclical nature usually takes place during the winter months (November to early March) when it is very cold here and there is no chance for working and earning here. During this period of male migration, women stay at their homes with their children and survive on the money which their men send them from outside Kashmir. On our inquiry about this matter, it revealed

TABLE 8.18

APPROACHING THE COURT FOR FAMILY DISPUTE

Sl. No.	Has anyone from your Family Approached Court in a Family Dispute?	Baramulla Men	Baramulla Women	Budgam Men	Budgam Women	Total Number	Total Percentage
1.	Yes	05	08	04	02	19	13.8
2.	No	95	142	96	14/8	481	86.2
	Total	100	150	100	150	500	100

TABLE 8.19

INITIATIVE OF GOING TO THE COURT

Sl. No.	*Initiative of going to court taken by?*	*Baramulla*		*Budgam*		*Total*	
		Men	*Women*	*Men*	*Women*	*Number*	*Percentage*
1.	Woman	04	04	04	01	13	69.6
2.	Man	01	03	00	01	5	25.2
3.	Both	00	01	00	00	1	5.2
	Total	05	08	04	02	19	100

that a significant number of males from the villages in Baramulla and Budgam districts (i.e. 26.31 per cent) go outside the state regularly for the sole purpose of earning money and feeding their families.

Table 8.20 reveals clearly that men from all villages migrate to the places which are located outside the valley and outside the state. At those places, these people work and send to their families. Moreover, most of them are in a position to save some money.

TABLE 8.20

PLACE TO WHICH PEOPLE MIGRATE TO WORK DURING THE WINTER MONTHS

Sl. No.	*Where Do they go*	*District Baramulla*	*District Budgam*	*Total*	
				Number	*Percentage*
1.	Within District	00	00	00	00
2.	Within the Valley	21	07	28	35.4
3.	Outside the Valley	05	11	16	20.3
4.	Outside the State	16	19	35	44.3
	Total	42	42	79	100

Movement of Females

Women in Baramulla and Budgam districts, like in other districts of the Kashmir valley, move freely outside their homes and their villages without any male companion. They also visit markets, hospitals, schools, offices, and so on freely and without any male companion. However, they take the male companion necessarily when they visit places located outside the valley and the state. This is clear from the information in Table 8.21.

Problems and Issues of Women in Kashmir

The above-mentioned findings related to the issues of women in Kashmir valley were presented in the seminar before the audience of academicians, bureaucrats, planners, women activists, representatives of local and national NGOs, researchers, experts, social welfare administrators and so on. Subsequently, these findings were discussed in detail and every finding was analysed critically. Finallly, the discussion about survey findings gave rise to two major points. Firstly, the

TABLE 8.21

PLACES WHICH THE RURAL WOMEN VISIT WITH AND WITHOUT MALE COMPANION

Sl. No.	Do married/unmarried female folk Travel without male Accompaniment to	Unmarried Girls		Married Girls		Total
		District Baramulla	District Budgam	District Baramulla	District Budgam	
1.	Neighbouring villages	45	102	105	148	400
2.	Health Centre Hospital	43	120	107	150	420
3.	Shops in the village	114	85	77	137	413
4.	Market outside village	35	37	85	87	244
5.	To Primary School	109	150	139	00	398
6.	To Middle and Hr. Sec. School	00	97	00	31	128
7.	To college	00	00	00	00	00
8.	To work	00	31	00	27	58

problems/issues, observed in the findings, were important and focussed on the crucial aspects of the women's life in Kashmir. Secondly, at the same time, these problems/issues were neither significant nor core problems of women in Kashmir. In fact, these problems/issues stood as secondary rather than primary problems/issues of women here. The participants felt that there was another set of problems/issues of women here which may be considered as core (problems/issues) and stood for primary importance. They also held that this set of problems/issues stood basic for the realistic and basic understanding of women's prevailing situation here. These problems/issues and their major aspects, identified by the participants, are as follows:

Attainment of Literacy / Education

The literacy among Muslim women in the Kashmir valley stood very low in comparison with the Pandit women, J & K State and national averages. As per the 1991 census/estimate records, the literacy rate among women in Kashmir province was 17 per cent in comparison with the literacy rate of 100 per cent among Pandit women and 26 per cent and 46 per cent of J & K State and national averages respectively. The 17 per cent figure for Kashmiri Muslim women may go further down because it includes the 100 per cent literacy of the Pandit women.

According to unofficial micro-level surveys conducted by State Resource Centre of Kashmir University, Srinagar in the areas of Zadibal (inhabited by the minority Shia Muslims), the literacy rate among women varies from 2 to 5 per cent. While the younger age groups have comparatively 5 or more literacy rate, the elder age groups have near-zero literacy rate. The situation of literacy portrayed in this and the preceding paras demands that continued systematic and organised efforts must be carried out by the official as well as unofficial agencies and organizations to make the full attainment of literacy full success.

Total literacy of women, especially belonging to the lower economic and social groups/communities and classes seems must for their emancipation. In this regard, while the planned efforts of governmental agencies/organizations are crucial, the organized and consistant role of non-governmental organizations stands important and highly desirable.

In the absence of 1991, decadal census in Jammu and Kashmir state, there is an urgent need to carry out micro as well as macro studies of women in Kashmir focusing on multi-dimensional problems directly or indirectly related to education.

Since dominant majority of women in Kashmir is illiterate, they have not been able to participate in and benefited by the processes of growth, development and modernization. So, in order to make them equal to men in role and status, they have to be involved in the emancipation processes through providing them literacy.

Since majority of the illiterate women in Kashmir are compelled to work in handicraft sector/s, they have to be provided necessarily the distance type of education and adult-non-formal education, for which there are enough institutions in the valley.

There is an urgent need to carry out a study with the objective to develop methodology for pursuing the programme of total education to women in a specific timeframe and for resolving various problems which may emerge in the way.

Employment

In the changing situation in which women came out of their homes in large numbers for getting education and performing regular-remunerative jobs, it seems necessary to provide them jobs in the public as well as private sector. This will provide solid material basis for women's emancipation.

In order to pursue the goal of total change and development among women in Kashmir, they need sound economic basis. This can be made possible only through giving them permanent jobs. This will make change and development a living reality.

Since women have faced limitations and problems throughout, they must be provided various benefits, including reservation in government and private services, in order to make them equal to their male-counterparts.

In the Kashmir context, women belonging to the upper socio-economic groups and classes have undergone significant degree of change and development. Now, the women belonging to lower socio-economic groups and classes have to be alleviated through reservation and other relevant methods.

Economic Independence

In order to make change and development among women in Kashmir purposeful and realistic, they have to be made economically independent. This must reflect in the women's behaviour inside as well as outside their homes. So, it emerges as a necessary component in women's total emancipation.

Economic independence for women needs regular and permanent income for them. This can be ensured by providing the permanent jobs in government offices and making available the handicraft work in their homes.

The economic independence of women demands their gradual reduction and finally total negation on their parents, husbands and others. This demands the relevant reforms and their serious implementation on the part of official and non-official agencies and organizations.

Discrimination and Harassment

The discrimination against women in Kashmir prevails at the societal as well as state level. While the former type of discrimination reflects in the family and other related situations, the latter type reveals in the laws and rules of the state. The legitimacy for both types of discrimination is derived from religion, culture, social structure and so in order to establish egalitarian social order, these and other types of discrimination have to be negated completely through formal and informal efforts.

There is a fundamental need to assess the inegalitarian social system. In order to debase this system, formal and informal actions are needed in the legal and social fields.

The existing laws which legitimize unequal treatment to women have to be identified, assessed and scrapped, and new laws have to be introduced based on the needs of the changing situation.

The customary laws, especially related to inheritance rights of women before and after their marriage, reflect a clear case of discrimintion against women in getting the share from their parental property. This is also in practice in most of the rural areas. On the other hand, the Muslim Personal Law, which ensures a certain share to women from their parental property, is not obligatory. Thus, the practice of discrimination against women in Kashmir continues. In this context, several experts suggested various changes in the existing laws to provide equity and justice to womens.

Women's rights, especially of those working outside their homes, must be protected in legal and other ways in order to establish an egalitarian set-up.

In their process of emancipation, the women belonging to all age groups faced the chronic problem of harrassment on the part of elders in the families and seniors in their places of work. Though this problem existed in the past, it has developed more intensity and new dimensions in the present situation, especially when women at large have opted for a career work outside their homes on regular and remunerative basis. In some cases, the women become the victims and kill themselves. Bride burning, attempt to suicide and so on are clear examples of the phenomenon of harassment of women, especially of younger age groups. This needs to be stopped completely and immediately through formal as well as non-formal steps.

Empowerment of Women

In the background of above-mentioned situation, the empowerment of women seems a must. It will not only emancipate some women to the position of power, it will also generate all-encompassing process of emancipation among other women. In actuality, it will ensure the process fully effective.

The process of empowerment must cover all fields of life, especially social, economic, educational and political. Certain degree of reservation in the law-making fora and law-enforcing agencies seems desirable. This will lead to the emergence of new role and status for the women in Kashmir.

Exploitation of Women

Women in Kashmir, especially in the rural areas, face systematic and continued exploitation at the hands of wholesalers, middlemen and proprietors of the handicraft centres. In the absence of fixed wages for the handicraft items like shahtoosh-shawl, carpet, papier-machi and wood-carving, the handicraft businessmen pay minimum wages to the working women and get maximum profit for themselves. This situation needs immediate intervention on the part of the government. On the other hand, the social initiatives are needed for making governmental intervention more effective and more relevant.

The special focus of governmental and non-governmental efforts has to be on the girl child working in various areas of the handicraft sector. Their condition seems miserable. It is important to note here that the welfare efforts for them have to be carried out in such a way that they do not become counterproductive. So, they may continue their work for the least hours. At the same time, they must be provided general and professional / technical education, which may help them to start the earning career. Both, governmental as well as non-governmental agencies/organizations must collaborate in this grand effort.

Problems of Working Women

Since women in Kashmir have started working outside their homes in large numbers on regular and remunerative basis, they face various problems which need immediate response on the part of the government and the society at large.

Within their homes, the working women face problems such as custody of child/children during the daytime, socialization of the child/children, maladjustment with in-laws family members, competition and conflict between family members, overwork due to double role (one within and second outside the family) and many other problems. These problems need to be resolved within the families concerned.

Outside their homes, the working women face problems which include harassment by senior officers in offices, full of tension and crisis situations, exposure to and interaction with unknown male colleagues, lesser time for family members and other near relatives, lesser time available for entertainment and so on. These problems need to be tackled within and outside the family framework.

Legal Rights of Women

Many participants observed repeatedly that women in Kashmir, especially belonging to the rural areas are ignorant about their rights related to their lives. So, there emerges a fundamental need to develop among women the legal awareness, especially related to their life situation. They argued that complete legal awareness among women will certainly contribute towards the broader process of gender equality. Special emphasis must be on crucial areas/problems of marriage, divorce, inheritance, *Mehr,* economic and social security, education, income, employment and so on.

9

RECOMMENDATION ON STRATEGY, POLICY AND ACTION FOR WOMEN EMANCIPATION

Strategy

1. It is important to always bear in mind that women are not a homogeneous mass, therefore, a segmented strategy is needed. The urban-rural, educated-uneducated, poor-rich and age-related differences must reflect in focused employment generation programmes for women.
2. It must be recognized that throughout the country, self-employment programmes for women have proved to be less than effective. Hence other ways of promoting employment and income generation for women will also have to be considered.
3. All employment programmes for women should take into consideration physical resources, women's unemployment level, their existing skills, infrastructure facilities, industrial and agricultural profiles of the region. Therefore, an effective employment strategy must be location specific.
4. Due to the land reform in early 1950s, in J&K state, most families had acquired a minimum tract of land for tilling and hence the valley was in a much better state nutritionally as compared to other states in India. However, it needs to be understood that many of the family farms have become marginal farms over this intervening period spanning four and a half decades and much of the population is now getting only 3-4 months of food from them. In view of this, it is important to focus on other economic activities to ensure

food security for people which alone can ensure good nutrition for them.

5. Integrated Community Development Scheme (ICDS) has to be strengthened. It is essential to grant the status of a worker to the Anganwadi worker, which alone can ensure that she has adequate motivation and a high morale to run the programme and the status within the village to impart nutrition education, round up support for community involvement and target gender discrimination against the girl child.
6. Awareness raising on social practices which result in malnutrition and undernutrition among women and girls within the family is vital and no efforts should be spared to highlight the special needs of women in this regard. Awareness raising on nutritional issues is also important so that traditional as well as modern practices with regard to balanced intake are maintained and adopted by families.
7. Special awareness drives aimed at women are necessary to increase legal awareness as well as awareness on issues relating to health, political rights, environment, etc.
8. Initiatives to raise awareness should not be dependent on governmental support alone, but should mobilize other resources as well.
9. Jammu and Kashmir state should set up a Women's Commission.
10. A Resource Centre for Women's Studies must be established in the Department of Sociology, University of Kashmir (organizers of the seminar). The Centre, which must be wholly financed by the state government, must respond:
    (i) to all research needs of the Women's Commission in the J&K state; and
    (ii) to all academic and non-academic research related to the women's studies in J&K state to be carried out by the teachers, research scholars and all others interested in this field.

11. Every effort should be made to spread awareness about women's legal rights. It is essential if women are to benefit from economic and other schemes meant for them.

12. Even though, trafficking in women is not as, yet, rampant in the valley, this menace is likely to spring its head with rising consumerism and some instances are already being reported in this regard. Strategy has to be evolved to protect women from this menace.

13. Atrocities against women are on the rise. For rape victims, special provisions are needed so that their dignity is not violated further by the investigation mechanism and they do not face further trauma from their experiences being made public. Rape trials should be held in camera. Cases of minor rape victims should be dealt with extreme sensitivity.

Policy

1. Women's work contribution in the field is not reflected in the official data where they continue to be labelled as marginal and non-workers in large numbers. It is important to ensure visibility to women's work. Textbooks and the government-controlled media need to be reviewed to highlight the actual role of women in the family and the society and not the role of a dependent being which is the popular stereotype. Further, surveys by the government and other agencies should take this into account.

2. There is need for group activity as well as for individual enterpreneurship among women and economic initiatives for women must not mechanically head for cooperatives and group formation.

3. A number of schemes have been formulated for women's economic activities by governmental and quasi-governmental institutions. Many are outdated and many are inadequate and unsuccessful. The very nature of schemes at present considered "appropriate" for women needs to re-examined and dynamic planning is needed to rescue women from traditional low paying occupations. For instance, with restoration of normalcy in the valley, it is inevitable that tourism and other industry will show a high growth. It is important to integrate women in these areas.

4. In the short term, undernutrition and malnutrition can only be addressed by supplementary nutrition programmes by the government. At present, the government needs to maintain universal supplementary nutrition programmes for different sub-groups.
5. The decision to restrict the mid-day meal scheme in schools has been hastily. This service can well serve the needs of the school going children. Other states are running the scheme successfully. Districts should be given the flexibility to try and evolve models to run the scheme and it should be continued on a universal basis.
6. Public Distribution System (PDS) has a vital role to play in providing basic food security to people. Targeting it to people below the poverty line will mean new malpractices and deprivation of other marginal sections. Instead the present system of economic graduation in Kashmir should continue and the PDS should give subsidized coverage universally to the remaining people.
7. There is a need to further enhance the facilities for doctors and paramedics in the rural areas so that they can concentrate on their work and do not constantly look for other avenues of employment. An additional incentive should be giving weightage to rural experience of doctors in P.G. admission. It is also important to focus on building and supporting village level expertise to deal with emergencies and common health problems as it will not be possible to ensure the presence of doctors in remote areas in the near future.
8. Health education and awareness is important, particularly in the areas of AIDS awareness and practice for safe drinking water.
9. Pre-natal care in rural areas to be improved. Knowing the nature of the terrain, innovative shemes should be devised to identify high risk pregnancies and to ensure hospital facilities for these women.
10. Given the adverse sex ratio, there is a need to ensure that the practice of selectively aborting female foetuses does not make inroads into the valley. Campaigns need to be

launched in this regard and monitoring committees need to be established in every town.

11. There is a need to encourage genuine, local and private initiative at various stages of education to supplement the efforts of the government.
12. Vocational component of education needs to be strengthened both in traditional as well as modern occupations.
13. Special provisions need to be made to rehabilitate divorced and widowed women who had married outside the state.
14. The state should make special provisions to rehabilitate all divorced women.
15. Discrimination is highly prevalent in matters relating to inheritance despite many court rulings in this regard. The government should take some bold steps to ensure that women get their due. Customary law in this regard which discriminates against women should not be allowed to take precedence over personal law.

Action

1. In order to release women from learning only the traditional skills such as cutting and tailoring, it is important to start more ITIs for women where they have a clear opportunity to undertake non-traditional courses.
2. Environment friendly wasteland development and fuel/fodder plantation schemes run women's cooperatives, need to be started in the rural areas. The energy policy has to be taken care of by rural women.
3. New schemes with women need to be undertaken in the area of agro-processing. The state government should provide necessary financial, technical and marketing support.
4. Plant allocation for women specific programmes should be enhanced. Without this, it is futile to expect that women's development can make a headway.
5. University of Agriculture should quantify the contribution of women to the agrarian economy.

6. Mahila Banks should be established.
7. A number of micro studies on following topics need to be carried out:
   (a) a study of gender discrimination in the Gurez block of Baramulla district;
   (b) recent trends with respect to wage employment of women and social perceptions in this regard;
   (c) women-headed households and their problems;
   (d) problems of widows and orphans; and
   (e) women in the service sector.

Alternative sources for funds for research were identified which included the UGC, Department of Women and Child Development (Ministry of HRD), ICAR, UNICEF (United Nations International Childrens Emergency Fund), National Foundation of India, UNFPA, UNIFEM and ILO (International Labour Organization).

8. Given the relative homogeneity of rural Kashmir, other than the absolute poor, vast sections of the population are above the poverty line but nowhere near prosperous. Hence ICDS should aim at universal coverage of 0-6 years age group and all pregnant and lactating women. The number of Anganwadis should be enhanced as one centre cannot serve the needs of 150-200 children meaningfully. The allocation of Rs. 1.5 per child per day is grossly insufficient to meet the desired norms of supplementary nutrition and needs to be enhanced. Mothers groups should be involved in preparing supplementary nutrition.
9. Health infrastructure needs to be enhanced. Provisions in the 9th Five Year Plan should be reviewed for sufficiency.
10. Introduction of user charges and the need to purchase medicine from the market has a negative impact on the health of women who have little control over cash and of most girls whose families are reluctant to spend. Women and girls should be provided free health care by the government.
11. There is a paucity of information about the incidence of diseases and even the incidence of breast cancer, cervical

cancer and reproductive tract infectious diseases is not known. It is important to ensure that diagnostic and treatment facilities for these problems are available at the district level.

12. HIV testing and counselling and support service for positive cases need to be established at the district level even though surveys have not thrown up many cases.
13. ANMs who have to be constantly on the move should not suffer from a sense of insecurity. A small beginning needs to be made to coordinate their touring with the field staff of other departments such as Gram Seviks.
14. Micro level studies and interpretation of hospital records are needed to provide focussed health care to women and girls. New health problems such as mental disturbances, peptic ulcers, hypertension, etc. have emerged recently. These need to be investigated and special measures need to be instituted to help people cope with traumas resulting from the turmoil in the valley.
15. The norms of providing a school within a kilometre has ensured that there is no dearth of schooling opportunities in the valley. Efforts have to be made now to improve the quality of education, infrastructure, teaching materials, facilities for curricular and extra-curricular activities.
16. Total literacy drives should be initiated within the state and adult education be made functional and operative. Women's education should also have an element of skill development and functional and social awareness.
17. Counselling and guidance services for women should be made available for women in the rural areas to deal with the problems arising out of the turmoil in the valley.
18. Women's leadership development programmes should be initiated in the state for effective leadership to emerge among rural women.
19. Legal cells should be set up in each district to ensure that there is no violation of laws enacted for the welfare of women.

20. Family courts should be established in every district to deal with matrimonial cases and the presiding officer should be a woman judge.
21. Limit of Rs. 500 per month under Section 488 Cr. PC should be raised keeping in view the financial status of the husband as well as the needs and the social status of the wife. There should be an amendment relating to jurisdiction so that women can file cases from their places of residence.
22. Suitable laws should be enacted to protect the legal rights of divorced women with respect of maintenance of children, ensuring return of dowry and payment of *mehr,* etc.
23. Recommendations of the National Commission for Women which gives Muslim women rights to adopt a child, seeks registration of marriages to prevent bigamy and setting up of counselling cells should be adopted by the state government.
24. Programmes to sensitize police officers, judiciary and the policy makers towards gender issues should be launched.
25. National Commission for Women should extend support to legal-literacy projects.

10

PRESS REPORTS ON NATIONAL SEMINAR ON GENDER DISCRIMINATION IN KASHMIR (1997)

Survey

Discrimination against Women Persists in Valley

From Massod Hussain

Srinagar, July 31: Kashmir's rural women have changed quite a bit in the last few decades and education has played a pivotal role in shifting their priorities. A survey on prevalent gender discrimination in Baramulla and Budgam districts has uncovered the fact that the discrimination persists in one or the other form in the conservative society.

Conducted by the Sociology Department of the University of Kashmir, the UNICEF is sponsoring a national level seminar on August 4, here. Some eminent experts and well-known personalities from UNICEF and prominent NGOs are scheduled to attend the seminar and help the state government, a co-sponsor, to evolve a consensus to change the status quo.

The survey was completed in the record time and the remote hamlets were covered in the testing times.

The findings are interesting and exciting. But in both the cases the crux is the same universally accepted fact that females are second to men and the society is male-controlled and normal survival is possible by following male-made decisions. Besides, the survey found the valley is not living in isolation and positive feminism has just started. There is no widow-cursing and the wife-bashing is not so alarming, the survey found.

Education

Using multiple methods of social research, the investigators interacted with 688 respondents, 90 per cent of whom felt there were no reasons to resist the attainment of education by both sexes. Most of them, however, said the boy's education is being favoured and preferred (by family), as they have to make themselves eligible for good earning and have to face tough competitions. Unlike youngsters, the elder-age and the religious oriented groups opposed equal education for boys and girls citing social, economic and religious factors. Poverty figured atop the list of factors which prevented parents from sending their siblings to school. This is followed by "no encouragement" and unfavourable environment by the state.

Family and Marriage

A dominant majority of 63.30 per cent respondents admitted their education helped them in marriage of their children but for two per cent it proved a hindrance. This "virtually ignorable" section was identified by researchers as "occupational communities". While 75.6 per cent respondents viewed the cooking as the girl-exclusive job, only 54.8 per cent felt the job of looking after the siblings is for the fair sex.

What is the ideal age for marriage for boys and girls in these two districts? The response was interesting.

For girls' marriage, the tender age of 18-20 age groups was preferred by dominant section of males in both the districts (47 per cent in Budgam and 29 per cent in Baramulla). Women themselves, however, said 23-25 age group was better stage for girls to marry (49 per cent in Budgam and 54 per cent in Baramulla).

For boys', it was 25-27 age group that was termed the ideal stage for wedlock by men (47 per cent in Budgam and 38 per cent in Baramulla). The women, however, differed on this front in the two districts. In Budgam 44 per cent women suggest 28-30 age group, a better stage for marriage but in Baramulla this age group was favoured by just one respondent as 47 per cent women, there, want grooms in 23-25 years.

As regards marriage of children, size of family, education to children both the sexes have equal rights with males enjoying slightly an upper hand. In purchases and sale of property and crops, the males have a monopoly.

As regards dowry, the study revealed that 82 per cent have given or will give the dowry at the time of marriage of their children and only 18 per cent disapproved of it. The dowry had its own fixation for the different classes. It ranges between Rs. 50-Rs. 100,000 in upper class, Rs. 30-Rs. 50,000 in middle class and for lower class it was around Rs. 25,000.

Though there is no hard and fast rule fixed rule for *Mehr* in Islam other than that it is to be paid, the society has simply fixed ranges in it. In lower group, it does not exceed Rs. 9,000, in middle income group it limits to Rs. 30,000 and in upper income groups it starts from fifty thousands.

Work Share

The survey found 62.8 per cent respondents revealed the family farming is done by women to earn money or help their families as 35.8 per cent felt the women work in the dairy activities and 10 per cent revealed the women are engaged as wage labourers. Men and women in the villages have an equal share in the work in various fields related to animal husbandry. It was an overwhelming 311 respondents out of 500 who said the women participate in all major outside economic activities. As regards property rights, males enjoy more rights than women.

Health

The survey found that less number of children were born in the families of the respondents as 67.3 per cent said they had one birth in their families in last three years. A dominant 76.2 per cent women, availed the services of hospitals during pregnancy. Though only 20 out of 300 respondents admitted they had an abortion, the surveyors said they had enough reason that the abortions were on a higher side as it carries social disapproval.

Inheritance

The surveyors were told by 65.4 per cent respondents that the women do not inherit her fathers property but the rest agreed the women enjoy the right. It was only 24.2 per cent who said the widows inherit their husbands property. In case of family disputes only 13.8 per cent approach the court and the initiative is taken by women as told by 69.6 per cent cases.

The survey has studied almost all the important sphere of activities of rural life and the participation by the two sexes. The voluminous report has discussed the issues threadbare. On the basis of the data collected by the researchers in the remote villages, the state government, the Sociology Department and the UNICEF have jointly organized a day long seminar on August 4, at the SKICC here. Prior to the seminar, four different groups of experts will discuss four major themes in light of these findings. They will make suggestions to the government, later.

A galaxy of important people are expected to participate in the seminar. These include Prof. Yugindra Singh (JNU), Prof. Noor Mohammad (AMU), Prof. A.R. Moumin (Bombay University), Prof. Gopal Ayer (Punjab University), Ms Mohini Giri (Chairperson National Commission for Women), Dr. Veena Muzmdar (Chairperson Centre for Women's Studies), Dr. Sarla Gopalan (Ex-Secretary Government of India), Ms Shashi Rajagopalan. UNICEF will be also represented. There are some senior academicians from Jammu and Kashmir. The entire survey was sponsored by District Administration Budgam and Ms Kalpana Mehta (SAHELI), Maitreya Ghatak (MODE) and Sundeep K. Nayak have been special contributors to the survey.

CM Calls upon Women to Fight Against Discrimination

ST News Service

Srinagar, Aug. 4—The Chief Minister, Dr. Farooq Abdullah has called upon women to assert their rights and fight against discrimination.

Inaugurating a national seminar on gender discrimination in Kashmir valley at SKICC here this morning, the Chief Minister expressed anguish over the plight of women in the country even when the civilization was at the threshhold of 21st century. He said though much was being said about women liberation, still a large chunk of them were subjudicated and exploited. He said the cruetly against women has not ended and cited the hanging of three Agra sisters who hanged themselves as their hapless parents could not meet the dowry demands. He urged women to ponder over this trend and wage a war against discrimination.

Expressing optimism about women getting rightful place in the society, Dr. Abdullah said they were not lacking talent or initiative but the only thing they needed most is direction which the women organizations could provide. He said the women have made significant strides in different spheres. Of late, the women are excelling in the field of education, he said and added that still enough is expected from them and their role in various fields cannot be undermined. He asked the womenfolk not to be disappointed as time is changing. What we require is change in attitude.

Conceding that women were not given their due share in the State and even in his cabinet, the Chief Minister said that his government sincerely believes in their upliftment and involvement in decision making. He said 33 per cent provision has been made for them in Panchayats. He said despite opposition from some quarters this historic legislation has been passed in Jammu and Kashmir while a merated several measures taken for their welfare. "We believe in co-existence of men and women and not in tension between them or exerting superiority of one over another", he said.

Speaking on the occasion, the Minister for Agriculture, Mr. Abdul Rahim Rather said a historic opportunity has been provided to the women of Jammu and Kashmir state by giving them 33 per cent reservation in the Panchayats. He said the amendment in the Constitution envisages that in case the women are unable to get their share in a particular Panchayat, their quota would be filled by nominations. The purpose is to solicit their involvement in the policy making at grassroots level. He said that this legislation is a landmark in the 50th year of India's Independence.

Mr. Rather emphasized the need for strict enforcement of laws enacted for safeguarding the rights of women and prevention of crime against them. He suggested that there should be a national debate on gender discrimination so that solutions are found to the problem.

Recounting the contribution of Kashmir women in historical perspective, the Minister recalled the spiritual and intellectual heights achieved by two sisters, Dehat and Behat, the disciples of patron saint Sheikh Noor-ud-Din Noorani. The works of Lalded in the literary landscape not only in Kashmir but in the entire world are considered as the only contribution of universal dimensions during the entire 13th and 14th centuries, the Minister said.

Mr. Rather said that tradition was kept up by Kashmir. It was symbolised through the romanticism of Haba Khatoon and in the mysticism of Arni Maal later.

These great ladies, he said, represent the grandeur of this place, the ethos of our land and the equality of opportunity this land provided to all for intellectual growth.

Mr. Rather noted with satisfaction that the agenda for change and welfare of women has set in the State and referred to various measures taken by Dr. Farooq Abdullah government in ameliorating the lot of women.

The Chairperson, National Council for Women, Mrs. Mohini Giri expressed the hope that the popularly elected governement would put women welfare on the top of its agenda and strive for their all round development. She hoped that the elected government of Dr. Farooq Abdullah would take concrete steps for ending gender discrimination by giving due representation to the women in State cabinet.

The Vice Chancellor, Kashmir University, Prof. M.Y. Qadri read the key note address. He dwelt on various aspects of the multifarious role of women both in traditional and modern societies and discrimination meted out to them in male dominated society. Quoting available studies, he said that women were not considered equal to men despite the fact that they work for longer hours than men. He, however, added that change among women in Kashmir started from the early decades of this century, especially from 1930 when the freedom movement started. Starting from speed of education, he listed many provisions of the Constitution and other legislations which guarantees rights of women as equal citizens.

The Chief Secretary, Mr. Ashok Jaitly, Financial Commissioner, Agriculture and Rural Development, Mr. H.H. Tyabji were also present.

The Daily State Times

Gender Discriminations

Srinagar, Wednesday August 6, 1997

Regardless of their rich contributions in every field the women of the state have failed to get their due place in the society. Despite the fact that they constitute fifty per cent of the total population their share in government jobs, semi-government organizations, autonomous bodies, private organization and even in legislature of council of ministers is not proportionate to their population. They do not enjoy equal rights as the menfolk enjoy. Their's is an exploited lot. Owing to religious reasons, may be their plight is not as sad as elsewhere. However, in rural areas the traditional laws inforce, have placed the women in a disadvantageous position *vis-a-vis* menfolk. They are denied their lawful share in the ancestral property. The element of poverty prevents them from receiving education. Their contribution in keeping the hearths of their homes burning, their role in agriculture and allied activities is no way less significant than that of their menfolk. In the urban areas the menace of dowry has made the life of women very miserable. Irony of the fate is that the womenfolk play a keyrole in the spread of the menace. There are thousands of girls who have been unable to find a suitable match because of the inability of their parents to raise huge sums to meet dowry demands of prospective grooms. Unemployment also comes in the way of the prospective brides to find suitable grooms. Apart from these social problems the women in the valley have been confronting a very trying situation since last eight years. They have become soft targets for guntotting men. A large number of them have fallen victim to the amours feelings of the gun wielding men. Their modesty has been more often than not sought to be outraged by the unruly gunmen. The government has on all the occasions, whenever the accusing fingers were raised against the security forces about their involvement, tried sabotage the due process of law. Contrary and transparency, it has done very little to substantiate it. The denial of access to the victims of atrocities for the neutral investigating agencies has adversely affected the credibility of the government. The case of withholding permission to the office bearers of National Commission for Women to examine the victims in the valley is the latest example of the official apathy towards the victims and its attempts at preventing the unravelling of the truth. If the government has nothing to hide, as it claims so, then it should have no objection to the National Commission for Women meeting the victims.

The overall situation for women in the valley is not good. Here social organizations, politicians and NGO's need to play their role to change the situation for women. The menace of dowry, which has been spreading fast, needs to be curbed at all costs. The people need to be made aware of the fallout of the menace and its disastrous consequences for the entire society. The gender discrimination witnessed in rural areas needs to be removed. The modesty and dignity of women needs to be protected at all costs. The criminals responsible for heinous crimes like rape or criminal assaults on women need to be exposed and brought to book. So that no woman is subjected to the humiliation of the worst kind in future. The women too need to get awakened to the situation. They shall have to put a bold front to the chauvinists, out to rob them of their respect and honour. They have a key role to play in fighting the menace of dowry. Similarly they can rid the society of other social evils which are threatening the very fabric of it.

Greater Kashmir

Gender Discrimination

Jammu, Wednesday, August 6, 1997

Chairperson of the National Commission for Women during her visit to state highlights the dire necessity of removing gender discrimination in J&K. According to her she is yearning for interacting with local women and have first hand feel of their miserable plight, particularly widows who lost their men at the hands of insurgents. She bemoans that it has not been possible due to security reasons and she has been prevented from visiting or interacting with them. It is not certain what is meant by security. There was an ugly episode as she entered the auditorium when she was extensively frisked. That chairperson of the NCW was herself subjected to such treatment is proof enough that gender bias manifests its ugliness abundantly in the state. Security is good, particularly when VVIPs are around, but overzealousy is quite abhorrent thought. It may be mentioned that Chairperson of NCW Dr. V. Mohini Giri enjoys the status of a Supreme Court Judge. By any reckoning she should have been allowed to go to local women for rational appraisal of the severity and magnitude of gender bias. By preventing her there is candid admission that such discrimination indeed exists and authorities do not like to open the Pandora's box for fear of some hypothetical hallucinations.

The fact that gender bias does exist is duly admitted by Chief Minister Dr. Farooq Abdullah. It is precisely because of this that state government envisages reservation of thirty three per cent seats in all Panchayats so that women become more assertive and gain sufficient clout to seek removal of prevailing discrimination. It is the simple case of disease being known but remedy remaining elusive. For that elaborate studies have to be carried out to see that feminity receives fair deal in every sphere of life. It is quite interesting that the discussions during the seminar raked up the topic of state subject rights of women married to men outside the state. Such women are automatically debarred from remaining state subjects. In other words, it is a curse to hail from J&K and the curse gets compounded if marriage is solemnised with someone from outside the state who is not a state subjects. Those defending the government side felt that any dilution of this course would erode autonomy and interfere with Article 370. It was also stated that maximum autonomy being sought shall also come under strain if this particular clause was deleted to remove gender discrimination. It must be borne in mind that state subject laws were enacted much before partition and there is simply no question of it having any bearing on Article 370. There is no law which remains immune from revision or update in conformity with the changed circumstances. In this context it is apt to mention that even Constitution from which all laws emanate has been amended over eighty times. It thus follows that this particular aspect relating to disqualification of women marrying grooms hailing from other states needs review. Some beginning is already made in that state government is amenable to let the disqualification become qualification in the case of divorcees or widows. It would be better to have an exhaustive study of the same and remove bias to the extent feasible.

It augurs well that the suggestion of NCW chairperson has been readily agreed to have separate Commission for women in the state. This is all the more important because NCW has no jurisdiction in this state. They can carry out studies through NGOs and other bodies but cannot compel the state government to follow its recommendations or go for enactment of the same. It needs to be appreciated that Dr Mohini Giri has offered substantial help out of the funds already earmarked under Ramoowalia plan for upliftment and education of women. It is equally nice of Chief Minister to do everything possible for removing gender bias at all levels. It is expected that formation of State commission for Women would go a long way in giving fair deal to the fair sex.

Daily Excelsior

Seminar Makes 55 Recommendations for Upliftment of Women

KT News Service

Srinagar, Aug 5: The day long national seminar on 'Gender Discrimination in Kashmir' concluded with the experts making as many as 55 recommendations to the state government for upliftment of women. The suggestions are the outcome of threadbare discussions made by 22 experts, forming the core group of seminar, on Sunday.

The recommendations fall under four major heads— legal rights of the women, men and women's work, nutrition and health, and literacy and awareness. The issues were identified as vital by the survey done jointly by the state government and the Department of Sociology of the Kashmir University. It was an UNICEF aided project.

The suggestions made on the legal rights front include setting up of state womens' commission, legal cells and family courts at the district level, special provisions for rehabilitating divorced and widowed women who had married outside the state, rehabilitation of divorcees, special laws to protect the legal rights of divorcees with regard to maintenance of children, bold steps to end highly prevalent discrimination in inheritance, to adopt the NCW recommendations with regard to registration of marriage and prevent bigamy, programmes to sensitise police officers, judiciary and policy makers towards gender issues and special provisions to be adopted by the investigators while dealing with rape.

The group comprising Ms V. Mohini Giri (Chairperson NCW), Ms Sushma Choudhary (Planning Commissioner), Ms Bala Jyoti (advocate from Jammu), Ms Gousun-Nisa Jeelani (judge), Ms Aasha Khosa (journalist), Ms Sayeeda S Hamid (member NCW) and Dr. Syed Mohammad Afzal Qadri (Law Department in the University of Kashmir) admitted that the atrocities against women are on the rise in the state. It also sought amendment in the section 488 CrPC that gives a divorcee a meagre sum of Rs. 500 for maintenance.

Another group which discussed the "Men and Women's Work" admitted that since women are not a homogeneous mass, a segmented strategy is needed in effective employment generation strategy which must be location specific, also. It recommended that the state run media must highlight the role played by women in society and family. The group comprised many experts including Dr. Bashir A Dabla and Sundeep K.

Nayak (two key functionaries of the seminar) besides Director Social Welfare Ms Tanvir Jehan and Dr. Veena Muzmdar.

The panel headed by noted intellectual and author Prof Imtiaz Ahmad deliberated upon the findings of the survey with regard to education. It said that the scenario on the education front in the districts of Budgam and Baramulla is grim and there is a dire need to improve infrastructure, teaching material and facilities besides encouraging the private institutions. It has suggested women's education should have an element of skill generation. The need of strengthening vocational component of education has also been emphasized by the panel members which included Dr. Madhosh, Dr. M. I. Parray, and S. Khursheed-ul-Islam. A number of routine recommendations have also been made by the panel on health and nutrition.

The seminar had three sessions. The inaugural session was addressed by the Chief Minister Dr. Farooq Abdullah, Agriculture Minister Abdur Rahim Tather and the Vice-Chancellor Prof. M.Y. Qadri. Rather emphasised the need for strict enforcement of laws enacted for safeguarding the rights of women and prevention of crime against them. He suggested a national debate also.

In the afternoon session, the findings of the survey was presented and the social scientists responded to the questions posed to them by the select audience, around 150. They said that the study has been done in the testing times and the researchers interacted with 300 women, 200 men, 100 adolescent girls, 22 village leaders, 22 primary school teachers, 22 Anganwari workers and 22 auxiliary nurse widows. The recommendations made by the four core groups were also read out to the audience.

The late afternoon valedictory session was presided over by the Mrs. Radha Rao. She said that the women's exploitation starts from her home where mother exploits her in different ways. Chief Secretary Ashok Jaitley said that Kashmir women enjoys a better socio-economic status than their counterparts in other states and the cases of rape and eve-teasing were unknown till recently. He said the land reforms have helped the women in a better way.

Sheikh Khursheed-ul-Islam, the co-ordinator of the seminar and one of the two main researchers of the issue, told KTNS that the seminar was a success. He said that the discussion made on the study and the recommendations are going a long way in helping to uplift the status of the Kashmiri women.

Dr. Giri not allowed to interact with women sufferers J&K to have separate Commission for Women

KT News Service

Srinagar, Aug 4: The Jammu & Kashmir government will have a separate Commission for Women and it will be established within four months. Dr. V. Mohini Giri, the Chairperson of the National Commission for Women (NCW) has mooted the proposal as the Commissions lacks the jurisdiction over the state and it has been accepted by the Chief Minister Dr. Farooq Abdullah.

Dr. Giri suggested the state level commission on the line of the NCW in her brief address to the UNICEF sponsored National Seminar on Gender Discrimination in Kashmir Valley, today. She also offered help to the state in setting up *Lok Adalats* exclusively for Women, speedy legal awareness programme for women and family courts for women with all women staff. She observed that gender equations have changed a lot here when compared to the period when she visited to the valley as a young bride.

It was during that visit she had an interaction with the then Chief Minister Sheikh Mohammad Abdullah.

The Chief Minister Dr. Farooq Abdullah, who inaugurated the seminar readily endorsed the suggestion and declared that state would soon examine the pros and cons of establishing such a commission at the state level. "I assure you that my government will leave no stone unturned in restoring the rights of women and give them representation in every sphere of life", the Chief Minister said.

Expressing anguish over the plight of women in the country even when the civilization was at the threshold of twenty-first century, the Chief Minister said though much was being said about womens' lib, still a large chunk of them were subjugated and exploited. He said the cruelty against women has not ended and urged women to ponder over this trend and wage a war against discrimination.

The Chief Minister said that the women were not lacking talent or initiative, but the only thing they needed most is direction which the women organizations will provide. He regretted that there is only one women in his 27 member ministry and promised a fair deal in the Panchayat elections where 33 per cent seats stand reserved for women. "We believe in co-existence of men and women and not in tension between them or exerting superiority of one over another', he said.

Later speaking at a press conference Dr. Giri said that setting up of an Autonomous Commission for Women at state level was of utmost importance. With setting up of such forum, the women in the state will get speedy redressal of their grievances. She also announced that one *Parvarik Lok Adalat* will be conducted in Jammu with the help of a women's organizations and efforts are on way to identify another group in Kashmir. In these family courts, the victim does not need the services of a lawyer and the dispute is decided in a single go. There have been as many as 140 such courts all over the country, she informed.

Dr. Giri regretted that her Commission had no jurisdiction over J & K state and thus, was unable to carry out any work here. About the atrocities committed against women in the trouble hit Valley, Dr. Giri told mediapersons that they wanted to do something, but were not allowed to move by the state.

"My heart bleeds for those affected women and I want to go to them, but nobody takes me", she said pleading mediapersons to help her. Dr. Giri said that she has no authority to take suo moto action because of legal constraints. "I asked that government officer (Sushma Choudhary) whether women are being raped here, she said no, there is nothing of this sort here", Dr. Giri told the press-persons.

Dr. Giri, however, announced that she has already identified some Non-Governmental Organizations (NGOs) whom we will like to visit Kashmir and brief the NCW on status of women in Kashmir. She as well as Dr. Syeeda S. Hamid, a member of the commission, admitted that they have gone through the reports of certain women civil liberty activists "but watching things oneself is different". Dr. Giri also announced that the commission being a member of the NHRC will ask them to send a fact finding team to Jammu & Kashmir state.

The NCW chairperson said that she was not permitted by her hosts to interact with the women and they even failed to give me the exact details of the children who were at the destitute home."It was really disheartening that they are getting just a sum of Rs. 15 for diet which is nothing", she observed. Dr. Giri, even offered state to get benefitted from the Rs. 250 crore Ramuwalia Scheme of education meant exclusively for the girl child.

The NCW chairperson called for launching a strong and forceful movement against alcoholism as, according to her it was one of the main contributors to the increasing crime against women. She said that the Commission had already succeeded in getting it banned in several states including Haryana and Andhra Pradesh.

"We know that total ban on consuming alcohol was not practicable, but there are certain steps which could be taken to check it". Dr. Giri said adding that the Commission has approached all the Chief Ministers in this regard and suggested some measures in this regard. The measures, she said, were not to issue more and more licenses, ban the country liquor which was also poisonous and avoid granting permission to liquor shops near schools and colleges. "We realise how difficult it is to ban it totally, but we want an alternative which would not destroy the families", she observed. She informed that the thirty per cent of women convicts in jails have killed their drunkard husbands.

The NCW Chairperson expressing her concern over the increasing crime against women said that in a recently held conference of state home ministers, the states have assured the commission that they would check the menace of crime against the women. She said that in the case of rapes, the NCW has suggested certain amendments in law, which include that the child victim should not be hauled up in court and no medical examination should be done to them. It has proposed in camera trial of cases in respect of rapes. Dr. Giri, said that in totality "we have proposed to review 25 laws which are not friendly to women".

On alarming increase in child prostitution, Dr Giri said that 60 per cent of prostitutes are children of the age group of 10 to 15 years. There are 2500 prostitutes in every district across India, she said adding that in Mumbai alone the number of prostitutes is 40,000, out of which 8000 are from Nepal and 15,000 from Bangladesh. Lambasting the politicians and businessmen for encouraging prostitution in the country, the Chairperson said that the Commission awareness campaign has yielded good results so far and the "mothers do not allow their children to go for prostitution now". They have realised and are co-operating with us now, she added.

Dr. Syeeda S. Hameed, member NCW said that so far the commission has made 213 recommendations to the central government for altering the status of the women. On the rights of women from minorities, Dr. Syeeda said that we do not want to touch the personal laws, but try to enlighten them further, she said that the Commission is trying to identify different groups in minorities who will take up the job.

"We work for social transformation and seek help from every quarter", she said. She said that there was need to employ more and more women on technological side so that they could do something for themselves. "At least 10,000 women scientists in Agriculture are jobless, give them work and send them to villages to come to the rescue of their own people", she opined.

KT News Service

Dr Giri Promises Justice to Women Victims of Valley

Srinagar, Aug 5: Dr V Mohini Giri, the Chairperson of the National Commission for Women (NCW) today selected two victims of violence in the capital city here and promised them that the Commission will fight to get justice for them. Her interaction with the local womenfolk was said to be "just a chance meeting".

Knowledgeable sources revealed the NCW group went to Dastkaar Centre, a handicraft centre run by some women volunteers at Khanyar. It was there that a number of women assembled within a few minutes and briefed the team about the plight of women in strife-torn valley. Those working in the centre also provided a lot of information to visiting dignitaries.

The women told Dr. Giri that they are being caught always in the crossfire though they were neither militants nor politicians. They pleaded that the "rude security forces" have always been creating harrassing them, which sometimes results in rapes during cordon and search operations. The women pleaded that their dominant portion across Kashmir is suffering from acute fear psychosis which sometimes results in different ailments.

It was from this mob of women that Dr. Giri identified two women, victims of violence and promised them all type of help in getting justice. The names of these women were not immediately identified, however, one of them is reported to have been tortured in a crackdown while another has lost her husband in firing by the security forces leaving her destitute with three children with no source of income. The NCW chairperson was there for about 45 minutes.

Earlier, speaking to the students and the teachers in the Law Department of the University of Kashmir in the morning, Dr. Giri called upon the fair sex to rise to the occasion and fight an organized battle to stop every type of cruelties. Reiterating that the special status of J&K does not permit her to do whatever the commission is doing across India, Dr. Giri offered the girl students an opportunity to get trained at the National Law School in the legal education with reference to women.

She also offered lady teachers from schools to join this legal awareness programme at the expenses of the commission adding that any number of women can join this programme. This is the only way to spread the awareness among common women about their rights with reference to the situation, she observed.

Briefing the gathering about the special programme about the minorities, Dr. Giri said that they have a special cell that exclusively works for the education of their female children and a control room has been set up to help the women in distress.

Responding to the queries after the lecture, Dr. Giri said that the commission lacks jurisdiction over Kashmir, but the women on their own, here, can form a network that shall brief the commission about the atrocities being committed by the conflicting parties. She also promised the women questioners that she will ensure that the NHRC people visit valley and meet the women who have suffered during strife.

Dr. Giri observed that the women should not be made the target of the violence by anybody especially because they are not forming a party from either side. Dr. Giri was told by the women participants that they are supposed to get killed in case they cry about the violations of human rights.

Kashmir University VC Prof. M. Y. Qadri while welcoming the NCW chairperson said that the Law Department of the University will take a lead in educating the women about the law governing their rights. He also said that the University will make the awareness programme part of the syllabus also.

Dr Giri concluded her three day visit and left for Delhi in the afternoon. She had come here to attend the National Seminar on Gender Discrimination in Kashmir which was jointly organized by UNICEF, the Sociology Department of the University and the Government of Jammu & Kashmir.

KT News Service

They Deserve a Better Deal in the Male Dominated World

Sheikh Zahoor

Srinagar, Aug 4: Women in traditional Kashmiri society have equally shared the sorrows and fortunes of common life. Her function and position has distinctly remained subordinate to men. Although the practice of infanticide, foeticide and dowry deaths were not resorted to in the traditional Kashmiri society, the prejudice against the birth of a female child lies there even today. While the Kashmiri women enjoy certain advantages available to them under Muslim laws, they equally suffer in many other areas of social life.

In the traditional Kashmiri society, women generally remained confined to their family and their world was their home. Not considered equal partners in their family life, the Kashmiri women were usually subjugated, discriminated and maltreated. Although their social role was minimal, they actively participated in the economic life especially among the lower socio-economic groups. In the urban areas, while the women of upper classes were completely confined to their homes and were not allowed to perform any manual labour outside their homes, the women belonging to various occupational groups worked with their men both within and outside their homes for earning a livelihood. But, despite this active economic role, the women were not given complete economic independence and higher social status, they deserved.

To address to these differences and highlight the problems of the Kashmiri women, a seminar on "Gender Discrimination in the Kashmir Valley" was organized here today. The seminar was jointly conducted by the Department of Sociology, University of Kashmir, UNICEF and the Government of Jammu and Kashmir. The seminar was based on the findings of a study undertaken by the Department of Sociology, University of Kashmir, on gender discrimination in two districts of the Valley—Budgam and Baramulla. The study was carried out to explore the reality of the gender discrimination prevailing in the rural Kashmiri society.

According to the findings of the study although the situation of gender discrimination prevails more or less in the entire Valley, the intensity of this phenomenon is more in the rural areas than in the urban areas. This difference, according to the study may be explained in terms of the broader and deeper impact of education, mass media, social and economic mobility and so on.

The study says that attainment of education has emerged as one of the significant factors for broader change among women in Kashmir. Consequently, the degree of illiteracy among women has reduced significantly. Even religion and culture are used to encourage the educational attainment of both the sexes. The study revealed that the attainment of education has affected the marriage patterns of boys and girls. The reasons cited for positive impact of education on marriage included getting a good match, increase in possibility of adjustment, increase in income, emergence of comparable role of women, encouragement of children's education, social mobility of the family, helpful during the period of pregnancy, child birth and child rearing and development of home management.

On the work front, the study reveals, that women in rural areas and in traditional situations are highly productive in the economic, social and other fields. According to the study, the women in the villages perform important works within and outside their homes. Regarding some important family decisions like marriage of children, the study reveals, that such decisions are taken by both the sexes, however, the males have an upper hand in this field.

The survey reveals that divorces are generally considered undesirable and are practised as the last resort. According to the study, support to the children after divorce is always borne by the ex-husbands and the women after divorce live with their parental families.

About the inheritance rights, the study says that there seems no uniform pattern of inheritance rights and most of the women are in favour of the share which their religion has kept for them and which is desirable to them.

The findings of the study are a pointer towards the emergence of a mass consciousness among women and men about women's rights in their homes and outside. The Kashmiri women have developed an interest and motivation to come out of their homes for education, employment and entertainment.

The Daily Greater Kashmir

Changes in State Subject law linked with accession

Srinagar, Aug 4: The hosts had a tough time last night while convincing the Chairperson National Commission for Women (NCW) and other outside experts that the changes in the state subject law of the state will strike at the core of state's accession with the Union of India.

Dr. Mohini Giri was of the opinion that the existing state subject law is discriminatory against the women especially because she losses her state subject status if she chooses to marry outside the state. The controversy sparked off in a group discussion on the issue "Kashmiri woman and her legal rights". The participants to the discussion were Ms. V. Mohini Giri (Chairperson NCW), Ms. Sushma Choudhary (Planning Commissioner), Ms. Jyoti Bala (Advocate from Jammu) Ms. Gous-un-Nisa Jeelani (judge), Ms Aasha Khosa (journalist), Ms. Sayeeda S. Hamid (member NCW) and Dr. Syed Mohammad Afzal Qadri (Law Department in the University of Kashmir).

Whether the Kashmiri woman should lose her state subject status— the issue virtually divided the entire group with the state planning commissioner, the judge and the Dean Students' Welfare on one side and all others on the other side. The group while defending the existing state subject laws told the other group that the state subject laws continue to be the same as were in the pre-partition era and any attempt to amend that law will harm the basis of accession which mostly revolves round Article 370. Their hosts already conveyed to the guests that the demand will neutralize the state's efforts to get the eroded autonomy restored.

The panel discussion, however, concluded with a consensus that those Kashmiri women who choose to marry outside shall have a right to get their state subject restored, if they are widowed or divorced outside the state. This has been recommended to the state government also as one of the four suggestions for the improvement in the existing status of Kashmiri women.

KT News Service

No Gender Discrimination

Srinagar, August 4: The State Government and its overzealous security network demonstrated today that they do not believe in gender discrimination. Atleast not in the matter of thorough frisking and body searches.

Even renowned women enjoying high positions are no exception as far as the frisking operation is concerned.

The Chairperson of the National Commission for Women Dr. V. Mohini Giri, who arrived here to attend the national level seminar on "Gender Discrimination in Kashmir" was not spared. She was subjected to bodily frisking and her belongings searched by the sleuths of the Chief Ministers security. Witnesses said Dr Giri was stopped by a police officer of the rank of the Dy SP, who was over-looking the SKICC hall, the venue of the seminar, before the arrival of Chief Minister, the chief guest of the function. Though, the elderly lady, enjoying the status of a Supreme Court judge, did not object, it was at the last moment that the organizers intervened.

The elaborate security arrangements had already created a headache for the organizers when they stopped Director Social Welfare and sent her back home. She, however, was later called back to attend the function.

KT News Service

State level Commission for Women in offing NCW to study women's suffering in strife-torn Valley

Excelsior Special Correspondent

Srinagar, Aug 4: Jammu and Kashmir would soon have a replica of the National Commission for Women (NCW) in a State-level Commission for Women as a suggestion to that effect has already been endorsed by Chief Minister Dr Farooq Abdullah. This was disclosed by the NCW Chairperson Dr. V. Mohini Giri at a press conference here today after a two-day seminar jointly sponsored by UNICEF's India Chapter, Kashmir University's Post-graduate Department of Sociology and the J&K Government on "Gender Discrimination in Kashmir Valley" concluded at SKICC this afternoon.

Dr Giri said that she had taken up the issue of the constitution of a State-level Commission for Women with the Chief Minister Dr Farooq Abdullah who, according to her, had agreed to establish the same in near future. NCW, due to the State's special status, has no jurisdiction over Jammu and Kashmir. Dr Giri said that in absence of jurisdiction, NCW was handicapped in formally conducting the study of the state of affairs afflicting the women in the border state. She, however, added that she would utilize the services of the research scholars and mediapersons to "indirectly" conduct the studies of the suffering faced by women in the militancy-torn State. "I am dying to go to the local women, but the authorities don't allow us to move for security considerations. I must come to know what afflicts the Kashmir women. My heart is bleeding for them," was the yearning of the NCW Chairperson who had no hesitation is saying that she had failed in her endeavour in the Valley due to the non-cooperation of the State authorities.

The women's rights activist asserted that in the capacity of her being a member of the National Human Rights Commission (NHRC) she would manage to send some of her colleagues to study the women's afflictions in Kashmir valley so as to suggest and implement the necessary remedial and rehabilitation measures. She said that for the same purpose she was currently in touch with a number of Non-Governmental Organizations (NGOs). Dr Giri said, in her tell-tale anguish, that she would like to go to the Valley interior, to interact face-to-face with the women of all hues "whether they belong to the families of militants or otherwise" and would also like to extend all the NCW support to the female victims of the turmoil. She said that she was highly concerned over the reported miseries of the widows of insurgency in the Valley. She said that she had enquired about the incidents of alleged rape and other excesses against the Kashmiri women, but the authorities, including the Financial Commissioner Ms Sushma Chowdhary had asserted that no such incidents were taking place in Kashmir.

Dr Giri said that NCW would extend the benefits of Rs 250 crore Ramoowalia national scheme for establishing schools for girl students to Jammu and Kashmir. She said that under the scheme a number of new schools would be set up exclusively for the girl students suffering of penury and other factors. She said that the discrimination against women in Government job opportunities could be judged from the fact that 10,000 Ph.D scholars in agriculture sciences were presently unemployed in the country. She said that due to the efforts of NCW for the last five years, as many as 140 Parivarik Mahila Lok Adalats had been established in India. No lawyers are engaged in such family courts. Besides 300 Panchayat training camps to inculcate legal education among the women had been set up. The girl students from all the colleges in India were being sponsored by NCW for getting legal education about the rights of women at National Law School, Bangalore. Dr Giri said that NCW had identified 25 laws "not friendly to women" and recommended the necessary amendments and annulments to the Government of India. It had, *inter alia,* proposed in-camera trial for all rape cases, exemption of medical examinations for minor girls raped and ignorance of character of the victim woman in all rape cases. She said that most of these recommendations had been accepted by the Central Law Commission. She said that in all 213 recommendations had been furnished to the Government by NCW and necessary follow-up action was expected in near future.

The NCW Chairperson stressed on employing all possible means to discourage alcoholism which, according to her, was the mother of all crimes in the country. She said that 30 per cent of the women detainees in jails had told her that they had murdered their husbands for committing upon them violence after consuming liquor and inviting their friends for sexual intercourse with their women. She proposed total ban on country-made liquor but admitted that only practicable measures could be used in most of the States.

Child prostitution in the country was the other areas of concern for Dr Mohini Giri, which, in her words, was thriving on "politicians-industrialists mafia." She said that 60 per cent of the sex workers at the brothels were girls between the age group of 10 to 15 years. She illustrated that 40,000 prostitutes in Mumbai were from the same tender age group. Dr. Giri claimed that sustained compaigning by NCW had brought about positive changes and the mother prostitutes were now keeping off their children from the brothels, NCW member Syeeda S. Hameed also spoke at the press conference.

The Daily Excelsior

'One woman in 27 ministers, 2 in 30 IAS officers'

Farooq Abdullah admits gender discrimination at all levels

Excelsior Correspondent

Srinagar, Aug 4: Chief Minister Dr. Farooq Abdullah has publicly admitted that there was gender discrimination in all spheres of life and all levels of the State in Jammu and Kashmir as well as all Indian States. He has stressed on sustained struggle to eradicate discrimination against the fair sex which, according to him, would never disappear in absence of a "full-fledged movement."

His expressions came during the course of his address at a UNICEF sponsored seminar at Sher-e-Kashmir International Convention Centre (SKICC) today. The Chief Minister on this occasion endorsed the suggestion of establishing a State level Commission for Women, earlier mooted by Chairperson of National Commission for Women Dr Mohini Giri.

Dr Abdullah candidly admitted that the equilibrium of the State dispensation in his own State was disproportionately tilted in favour of the masculine gendre and the fair sex had just a nominal representation both in his Council of Ministers as well as the top echelons of the bureaucracy.

He said that he had only one women in 27 Ministers while as Ms Sushma Chowdhary and Mrs Kotwal were the 2-odd ladies among the battery of 30 IAS officers. "But what can I do? This is an all-pervading phenomenon in the entire sub-continent," he hastily remarked.

Dr. Abdullah responded positively to the suggestion of Dr Mohini Giri that Jammu and Kashmir State should formulate its own State Commission for Women as the NCW had no jurisdiction over the State. Dr. Abdullah declared that his Government would soon explore the possibilities of establishing such a Commission and pros and cons of the Chairperson's suggestion would be considered favourably.

LIST OF MEMBERS OF THE CORE GROUP OF EXPERTS

Dr. (Mrs.) V. Mohini Giri
Chairperson
National Commission for Women
New Delhi.

Professor M.Y. Qadri
Vice Chancellor
University of Kashmir
Srinagar.

Dr. (Mrs.) Sarla Gopalan
Former Secretary
Department of Women and Child Development
Ministry of Human Resources Development
Government of India
New Delhi.

Ms. Sushma Choudhary
Commissioner/Secretary (Finance)
J&K Government
Srinagar.

Dr. (Mrs.) Sayeda S. Hameed
Member
National Commission for Women
New Delhi.

Professor Imtiaz Ahmad
Director
Academy for Third World Studies
Jamia Millia Islamia
New Delhi.

Professor A.G. Madhosh
Dean
Faculty of Education
University of Kashmir
Srinagar.

Professor Dost Mohammad
Department of Economics
University of Kashmir
Srinagar.

Professor A.H. Matoo
Director
Centre for Central Asian Studies
University of Kashmir
Srinagar.

Professor M. Afzal Qadiri
Department of Law
University of Kashmir
Srinagar.

Dr. Bashir Ahmad Dabla
Head
Department of Sociology
University of Kashmir
Srinagar.

Sundeep K. Nayak
Development Commissioner
District Srinagar
J&K Government
Srinagar.

Mr. K.M. Wani
Additional Secretary (Agriculture)
J & K Government
Srinagar.

Mr. M.M. Bhat
Director
Department of Rural Development
J&K Government
Srinagar.

Mrs. Puran Surana
Principal
Government Girls College
Rajasthan University
Jaipur.

Ms. Tanveer Jehan
Director
Department of Social Welfare
J&K Government
Srinagar.

Ms. Gousia Nissa
Sub Judge
District Srinagar.

Dr. M.I. Parry
Associate Professor
IMPA
Srinagar.

Ms. Asha Khosa
Correspondent
Indian Express
Jammu.

Mr. Maitreya Ghatak
C/o MODE
Calcutta.

Ms. Kalpana Mehta
C/o SAHELI
Pune.

Ms. Jyoti Bala
Advocate
J&K High Court
Jammu.

Ms. Shagufta Parween
Secretary
J&K Social Welfare Advisory Board
J&K Government.

Dr. (Mrs.) Aneesa Shafi
Department of Sociology
University of Kashmir.
Srinagar.

S. Khurshidul Islam
Department of Sociology
University of Kashmir
Srinagar.

LIST OF RESEARCH INVESTIGATORS OF THE SURVEY

1. Chief Investigator	:	Dr. Bashir A. Dabla
2. Field Supervisor	:	S. Khurshidul Islam
3. Research Investigators	:	Mohammad Amin Bhat
		Peerzada Mohammad Amin
		Nisar Ahmad Mir
		Roubina Kousar
		Hakim Nazir Ahmad
		Manzoor Hussain
		Tahira Hameed
		Muzaffer Ahmad Bhat

INDEX

Abortions
among women
number of in
Baramulla/
Budgam districts, 128
selectivity in
and monitoring, 177

Acts enacted to
remove gender
discrimination, 20-21

Agriculture and fruit
growing fields
—activities performed, 108-09
classification of works
related to, 110

AIDS—
attention to spread of, 17
awareness, 176

Anaemia among women, 16

Animal husbandry
classification of activities,
111-13

Articles in Constitution
forbidding discrimination, 20

Attitudes towards feminine
and masculine work, 105

Battering of women, 16

Baramulla district—
sample, 53
profile, 59
educational institutions, 1996, 71-72

Beijing Fourth World
Conference on
Women, 21
deliberations, 21-22

Benet Mary K.,
on women's jobs, 47

Biological division of
labour between
sexes, 15

Birth rates in
Baramulla/Budgam
districts, 126

Bowlby John
on role of women, 43

Bruno Betteheim
on continuous mother
child relationships, 44

Budgam/Baramulla
district
enrolment of students
in educational
institutions, 73
enrolment in womens'
polytechnics, 75
number of teachers in, 76-77

Budgetary allocation
for education, 76-77

Budgam district—
sample, 54
profile, 54

Caplow Theodore
on relegation of
women to
bottom, 47

Change in
position of
women in
India, 29
in Kashmiri
women, 19, 35

Children born in
family number
of in Baramulla/
Budgam districts,
126

Child survival
after birth, 129

Children's support/
custody after
divorce, 151-52
pattern of financial
support to, 152
reasons and criteria
for support, 152

Conduct of delivery of
children, 131

Control over different
assets
and status/
authority, 118
by men/women, 119-20

Condition of women
(present), 13

Counselling
services for
women, 179

Cross-cultural societies
women in, 41

Customary laws
and legitimacy
to discrimination,
169

Decade for women
programme (UN), 25

Decision making
pattern of
—by men and
women, 121
in family, 122-23

Destitute women's homes, 81, 86
functioning of, 86

Discrimination, 25
and harassment
against women, 168

Disqualification of women
marrying grooms hailing
from other states
review of, 190

Divorce—
in Kashmir, 32
to women, 135
and payment
of *mehr*, 136
incidents of, 137
reasons of, 139

Different types of work done
by boys and girls, 100-01

Dowry practice in Kashmir
society, 133

DWCRA
beneficiaries, 1991-94, 82-83
scheme, 124

Ease of divorce
for husband, 147
for wife, 148-49

Economic and educational
mobility in Kashmiri
women, 19
results of, 19-20

Economic independence, 168
demands of, 168

Education
development in J&K, 67
findings/opinion
regarding, 182
reasons for not
going for, 98-99

Educational institutions
in Budgam district,
1996, 70

Egyptian and Byzantive
queens and political
authority, 23

Emancipation of
Kashmiri women, 19
women in India, 28

Employment of women
in Kashmir, 167

Empowerment of women
in Kashmir, 169

Equal share of
women in
parental property, 156-57
question regarding, 159

Exceptions to women's
dependence on men, 23

Exploitation of women in
Kashmir, 170

Family
and marriage
findings/opinion
regarding, 182-83
disputes, 159
— regarding property, 159
— and approaching
courts, 162-63
—initiative by men/
women, 163
farming—by women, 105

Farooq Abdullah's
declaration in seminar, 1, 89, 193

Female dependancy, 30

Feminine works, 105

Feminism, 23
rise of, 24

Friedl Ernestive
on male
dominance, 45

Funding for research
on women
alternative sources, 175

Gender
bias—correcting of, 15
—in subcontinent, 15
meaning of, 39
stratification,
discrimination, 40

Gender discrimination
repercussions
study of, 40
phenomenon, 40
views on, 41

Global level
women in, 27

Group
activity—
need for, 175
of experts—
list, 207-10

Hacker Heben Mayer
on women in
minority groups, 49

Handicraft centres/trades
persons in, 84

Health

centres/facilities
available, 78-80
facilities utilized
during pregnancy, 127
facilities—
conditions in
Kashmiri society, 125
to men and women, 125
education and
AIDS awareness, 176
status of women
in Kashmir, 126

HIV (Human Immuno
Deficiency Virus)
spread of, 17
testing and
counselling, 179

ICDS (Integrated
Community Development
Scheme), 174

Impact of education
on marriage
practices, 97

Indira Mahila Yojana, 21

India
women in, 28

Inheritance rights, 153
of women in
Kashmir
from parental
property, 155, 184

Inheriting husband's
property by
widow—
pattern, 159-60

Industrial revolution
and women's
independence, 24

Interaction with
women sufferers

and prevention of
Mohini Giri, 193

Justice of women
victims of valley, 196-97

Kashmiri women
suffering of, 17-18

Kashmir
women in, 30

Legal rights
of women, 171

Legitimacy to
discrimination—
gives of, 168

Lionel Tigers and
Robin Fox on
gender discrimination, 41

Literate/illiterate
population, 198
in Baramulla/
Budgam
district, 64

Literacy/education
attainment in
Kashmir, 166-67

Maltreatment of
women, 31

Male/Female
and Rural/Urban
Population, 1981,
63

Marriage age for
boys and girls,
103-04

Marx and Engels
on women's
liberation, 50

Mahila Samridhi
Yojna, 21

Masculine works, 105

Medicines used by
women during
pregnancy, 130

Mehr
payment of, 134-35,
180

Men and women's
work and
employment
strategy, 191

Migration pattern
in Kashmir, 161
places where
people migrate, 164

Militancy situation
effect of during
child birth, 137

Modern education
development of
in Kashmir, 91

Mohini Giri, 189

Movement of women
without male
companions, 164-65

National Commission
for Women, 180,
188-89

Number of children
born—findings
regarding, 183
survived after
birth, 129

Nutritional health
and status of
women, 14-16

Oakley Ann
on division of

labour by sex, 43
on gender roles, 44

OBC/SC-ST
scholarships, 89

Occupation of
population Sex-wise, 69

Old-Age Revision
Scheme, 87

Orther Sherry
B.,
on universal
devaluation
of women, 46

Out of home
economic
activities, 114
attitudes towards,
114-15
priorities—
job-wise, 115

Parkin Frak
on inequality
of sex and
class status, 49

Patterns of inheriting the
husband's property
by widow, 159

Payment of dowry
during marriage, 133

Panchayati Raj Act,
1993, 21

Place of birth of children, 132

Place of residence
after divorce,
149-50

PDS (Public
Distribution
System), 176

Political authority
in women, 23

Polygamy
prevalence of, 31

Post-independence
developments, 34

Population in J&K
1991, 59
Budgam/Baramulla
—pattern, 1951-91, 60

Policy recommendation
for women's
emancipation, 75

Practice of wife beating,
153

Preference for
girls education, 92-93
boy's education, 94-96

Prem Nath Bazaz, 18

Programme for
women welfare, 34

Problems of women
in Kashmir, 35-38
social and economic, 36
educational, health
and discrimination, 37-38

Problems and issues of
women in Kashmir,
164, 166

Property Rights of Women, 32

Purdah
practice in woman, 33

Rashtriya Mahila Kosh
setting up of, 21

Recommendations for
women uplift, 190

Religious composition of
population in Baramulla/
Budgam districts, 65

Remarriage of
divorcees and
widows, 138
factors of, 138

Remarriage of
men after divorce, 140
—reasons, 139

women after divorce, 141
—reasons, 142
women after death of husband, 143
men after death of wives, 144
widows after death of husbands, 146

Research investigation of
—survey, 211

Resource Centre for Womens Studies, 174

Research investigators of survey, 211

Reproductive tract investigation in women, 17

Rights of women
consciousness of, 35

Role and status of women, 27
in traditional society, 13

Rural Development Programme of Women, 21

Self-esteem (low)
in women, 17

Seminar
organization of, 55

Seminar on gender discrimination, 1997
Press Reports, 181-206

Share of females
in parental property, 156

Sociological studies
on women, 14

Social welfare schemes, 80-81

Social role of Kashmiri women, 18

Socio-political movement and women, 34

Status of women
seminar, 1995
Budgam, 25

State subject laws
for Kashmiri women, 190

Study aim of, 25
nature, universe, respondents, methods, 51-52

Strategy for women emancipation, 173

Survey—
limitations and difficulties, 56-57
on prevalent gender discrimination, 181

Talcott Parsons
on gender discrimination, 42

Traditional trap of women, 28

TRYSEM Scheme, 124

UNICEF's *The Progress of Nations,* 16

UNICEF—
draft of survey submitted to, 55
sponsoring seminar, 181

United Nations Commission on the Status of Women (1946), 24

Unemployed persons
registered, 85

Urbanization in J&K, 66

Violence against women, 16

Vocational Training Centres and Courses, 87-88

Vocational components
in education, 177

Wife beating, 153-54

Women's empowerment—
initiatives taken for, 21

rights, 23, 169
commission, J&K, 174
liberation, 50
share in parents
property, 158

Women in Kashmir, 31

Working hours
rural women, 14

Working force
population in
Budgam/Baramulla, 67
number—by sex, 68

Works performed
by men and
women, 106

Works done by
women to earn
money, 116
—attitude towards,
nature of, 117

Working women
problems of, 170

Work share
men/women, 183